RICH & DONNA

THANKS FOR ALL

YOU DO,

Jim & Lynda

HOLDING GOD IN MY HANDS

*Personal Encounters
With the Divine*

Also by Paul Wilkes

In Due Season: A Catholic Life

Best Practices From America's Best Churches

Excellent Catholic Parishes

Beyond the Walls: Monastic Wisdom for Everyday Life

In Mysterious Ways: The Death and Life of a Parish Priest

Merton: By Those Who Knew Him Best

The Education of an Archbishop

These Priests Stay

Paul Wilkes

....

HOLDING GOD
IN MY HANDS

*Personal Encounters
With the Divine*

Liguori
LIGUORI, MISSOURI

Published by Liguori Publications, Liguori, Missouri
To order, call 800-325-9521 or visit www.liguori.org

Library of Congress Cataloging-in-Publication Data

Wilkes, Paul, 1938-
  Holding God in my hands : personal encounters with the divine / Paul Wilkes. — 1st ed.
    p. cm.
  ISBN 978-0-7648-1945-2
  1. Lord's Supper. I. Title.
  BV825.3.W55 2010
  234'.163092--dc22
  [B]

                                                              2010020282

Liguori Publications, a nonprofit corporation, is an apostolate of the Redemptorists. To learn more about the Redemptorists, visit Redemptorists.com.

Printed in the United States of America
14 13 12 11 10   5 4 3 2 1
First Edition

Contents

Introduction

Early each Thursday morning for more than a decade, I've parked my car in a sprawling lot, mounted concrete steps, and passed through a revolving glass door to enter a world where illness, pain, and disease preside. Except for those paid to be here—and those with rhythmically contracting uterine muscles—no one comes to this place willingly.

This is my local hospital. I am neither a doctor nor hospital employee, nor am I visiting relative or friend. A small, unobtrusive black leather pouch at my waist contains the reason for my visit. Within that pouch is God. And the purpose of my Thursday morning visits is to bring that God to people lying in beds in their numbered rooms, along well-lighted corridors, on the nine floors above.

I am what is called in the Catholic tradition an extraordinary minister of holy Communion, although I am hardly a "minister" at all, having had no more theological schooling than a few college classes and no seminary training. In fact, I have a very checkered past—wretched sinner, fallen-away Catholic, once divorced, for too much of my life a venal, proud, arrogant man. Yet I have been entrusted to carry God to them, a God in a tiny, pale beige piece of unleavened bread, the holy Eucharist or holy Communion. Perhaps the failures in my own life put me in an ideal position to come here each week. No one I will meet on my rounds is any less worthy than I am. They are the teachers; I will learn from them. Life lessons.

It is fundamental to Catholic belief that God, in the person of Jesus Christ, is present in each host, this holy Eucharist which is consecrated at Mass. The Eucharist is one of Catholicism's seven sacraments, the others being baptism, confirmation, reconciliation (or confession), matrimony, holy orders (ordination of a deacon, priest, or bishop), and the anointing of the sick. Each sacrament has a purpose: to bring down God's power and graces in response to a specific need or a new chapter in our lives.

Although all Christian traditions celebrate the Eucharist, most Protestant churches observe this liturgical service as a symbolic remembrance of the Last Supper. The Catholic tradition is more literal. The host is the Real Presence—the unambiguous term and teaching of the Church—of the risen Jesus Christ, no longer bound by the constraints of his earthly life, to be present at this time and in this place. Other Christian traditions do not take the Eucharist to the sick, preferring the healing power of prayer and Scriptural readings.

And yet, in the early Christian church, the Eucharist was the ordinary sacrament of healing. The early Christians knew no better way to bring comfort to the sick than to offer them the intimate presence of the risen Christ. It was as common a practice as bringing sustaining food or a medicinal cure. At the Last Supper, when the Eucharist was instituted, Christ promised to be with his people whenever they broke this bread and partook of it. And so, the Eucharist brought this "real presence" to those in need of healing.

I do not fully understand the doctrine of *transubstantiation*, the proper term for the change of unleavened bread into the Body and Blood of Jesus Christ. It's a mystery. But I know it to be true. I know it within my own life and through the experiences of the people I have visited and learned from, now some four thousand of them.

For this hospital—this place of agony, terror, and death—is also a place of grace, comfort, and healing beyond what medical science has or ever will provide. The Eucharist is not the result of alchemy or some sort of magic, conjured up, imagined, or hoped for by us mere mortals. It is simply an unvarnished truth: the real presence of God. God is present in that host. And receiving God in that host heals in ways beyond human understanding. I have seen miracles happen enough times as I brought holy Communion to patients here to know that something outside my control or will or hope has occurred.

Later I will tell of my own training, but in general, extraordinary ministers of holy Communion came into being after the Second Vatican Council (1962–1965), which broadened and deepened the role of the nonordained or layperson.

It's common for Catholics to use the terms Eucharist and Communion as synonyms, but canon and liturgical law are careful to distinguish between the two terms. Communion refers to the consecrated bread and wine. Eucharist refers to the act of consecrating the bread and wine and, by extension, celebrating Mass.

In March 2004, the Congregation for Divine Worship and the Discipline of the Sacrament published an instruction titled *Redemp-*

tionis Sacramentum: On certain matters to be observed or to be avoided regarding the Most Holy Eucharist which clarifies that the name *minister of the Eucharist* properly belongs to priests and bishops.

Ordinary ministers of holy Communion are bishops, priests, and deacons. Deacons fulfill their ministerial office when they administer holy Communion, even though they can not consecrate the bread and wine.

Redemptionis Sacramentum further clarifies that a laymember of Christ's faithful who has been delegated to administer Communion is referred to as an *extraordinary minister of holy Communion*, not the commonly used "extraordinary minister of the Eucharist" or "eucharistic minister."

Originally, an extraordinary minister of holy Communion not only assisted the priest in the distribution of Communion at Mass, but also took the consecrated host to members of the community who were not present at Mass because of ill health. Since then the role has been widened to take in all Catholics in a hospital—in this case, whether or not they are members of my parish—or any parish at all.

I entered into this work seriously, reverently, and—looking back—somewhat clinically. My weekly logs from those early months read more like medical charts than pastoral visits. Diabetes, amputated toe, radioisotope, CT scan, chemotherapy regimen. I wanted to know the "state" of my patients so I could better serve them in that visit and, for those with chronic illnesses or conditions, in the weeks ahead. Or so I believed.

I slowly began to realize the fuller impact of my visits, which mattered and which was less important. Yes, my patients needed an empathetic ear about their medical condition, but it was inner healing that they openly or obliquely sought. They wanted to be assured that God was standing with them, to feel God's comfort. They wanted to be physically healed, but lacking an immediate, miraculous cure wanted in some way (and this would differ widely) to know God's power and person in a tactile way. And that was exactly what I, flawed courier that I was, might provide. I was bringing God to them, and I needed to transmit as best I could what that actually meant.

So I began to ask less and less about their illnesses and more and more about them. If I was to serve them as individuals, I couldn't offer the Eucharist in some routine, generic way. I needed to see who was in the bed, what their life had been before this hospital stay, what was weighing heavily upon them, and what barrier—if any—they had erected that kept them from a holy, wholesome, trusting relationship with God.

People's lives are messy. Decisions inadvertently result in bad marriages. Too often, people are unwilling to forgive themselves. Sins weigh heavily; fear and guilt haunt and paralyze. Some feel outside the Church and God's love. Others are so hurt by something they ascribe to the Church—whether real or imagined—that they want nothing more to do with it.

In this messiness and misunderstanding, the Church—and extraordinary ministers of holy Communion—comes to them. And we who will have this profound opportunity in only few fleeting moments must make pastoral judgments, trying as best we can to discern how best to deal with them in their weakened and vulnerable states.

I will explain later the absolutist guidelines I was given. If I had adhered strictly to those guidelines, many—perhaps even the majority—of the patients I visited wouldn't have met those standards.

There is a letter of the law and its spirit. There are printed guidelines and the human being lying in a bed. In those few moments with each patient, I constantly had to make decisions about what to do, what to say.

I knew the guidelines. I also was guided by the words of Christ, who put more stock in forgiveness than in justice or punishment and the words of my beloved Pope John XXIII, whom I was able to see at St. Peter's in Rome just about the time the Second Vatican Council was opening. In his opening address to the council, he said the Church must "make use of the medicine of mercy rather than that of severity" because the Church—through the council—wants to act as a loving parent toward everyone, including those who are separated from the Church.

I took the words and intentions of all three into the rooms I visited.

I needed to make provisions and allowances for whatever obstacles or life circumstances stood in the way of their relationship with God. For my job was not to reorient or rectify their lives, or demand that they immediately turn to what might be considered full Catholic practice. In the short time I would spend with them, my job was to unite or reunite them with the living God who, if my own life and experience are any measure, readily brushes aside our failings to take each of us in his loving arms, especially when we are in need—which is certainly the case when we are in a hospital.

And now, please come along with me to learn these life lessons and see for yourself. The circumstances of the patients in this book are true, only their names have been changed to preserve their privacy.

The Pietà

The blazing red card on the door warned people who entered must wear gown, gloves, and mask. This signals a bacteriological two-way street, and I never know what direction I might be headed in. Am I the possible source of infection, or do I risk being infected? A pale young man lay almost flat in the bed, listlessly watching one of the morning talk shows, just then with great seriousness probing the message behind the hemlines at the spring fashion shows in Paris. The young man's skin was a strange, translucent, almost mustard color. There were a few spots on his forehead that looked like bruises, as if he had been in an accident. A woman, who I would later find out was his mother, sat next to the bed, closer than was usual. Although I wore gown, gloves, and mask, she did not. It was obvious she wanted no such barrier between them.

I don't always ask what has brought a person to the hospital, only when something in the room, or the look of the patient, or some instinct that I can never quite explain prompts me to inquire. This time I didn't need to ask. The story unfolded all too quickly. Dan was a local kid, graduated from one of our high schools fifteen years before. He wanted a bigger life than our provincial southern city could offer, so he headed for New York. He loved the life there, free from hometown inhibitions and the teasing and bullying he had grown up with because of his effeminate ways. While his career as an artist might not have taken off exactly as he had hoped, in the anonymity of the city he found a circle of friends and acquaintances, a community that understood and accepted him for what he was.

And there, AIDS would find him.

He knew all the gay bars in the West Village, and one day proudly walked into the Stonewall, famous for the police raid that helped launch the gay rights movement. He felt he had taken his rightful place in the world. At first, his new life was exhilarating, he told me, his voice flat and expressionless. Sex was negotiated and transacted in minutes: the more often, the more anonymous, the better. Then he found someone he deeply cared about, but in the tragedy that too many gay men experience, their past preempted a future together. By the time his lover died of AIDS, they were down on their luck and far behind on rent.

He had come back to the city of his birth to die. He said it without a trace of self-pity, as if he had come home to retire and spend many more peaceful years. No, church hadn't been a big part of his life in New York and, well, no one had asked him lately. I told him I brought holy Communion to patients and asked if would he like to receive. He said he would, but he was having trouble swallowing.

His mother had said nothing up to this point. She was a neat package of a woman, in her mid fifties, with precision-cut bangs and hair cut to just below her ears, set back by a pair of barrettes, a style now out of fashion. It was not hard to imagine her as a teenager with the same haircut. Her face was unlined except around her eyes. There, the years and the pain showed in faintly wrinkled skin, darker than it should have been.

I came closer to the bed and began to pray. "Lord, here we are, Dan and his good and caring mother, bowing our heads in your presence. Hold this good young man in your gentle embrace. Let him feel your love, your presence. Has he been away from you? No, not that far, if at all. And you, you Lord, have been close to him, through everything, through the good times and the not-so-good times up in New York. And now Dan has come back to be with his mother. And here she is, at his bedside, just like when he was a little boy, loving him desperately. Just as desperately as you do."

Holy Communion. That is what I was about to offer Dan. We use that term so often, it could lose its meaning, its power. Communion: to be one with. But a holy union. Dan had many unholy communions. Yes, all of us want to satisfy our urges—but more than that, I think it is a deeper desire to feel at one with someone who cares about us because by ourselves we feel so alone, so incomplete. This was so different. Here in this tiny piece of bread was true Communion, joining with the God of the Ages, the friend who never abandons, the Father who always seeks what is best for us.

What strikes me at moments like this is the patience of God, the hand always extended, even as we grasp for that completeness in so many foolish ways. I had once believed differently, that God's patience did indeed know bounds, that at some point, enough would be enough and I would be plunged into darkness. No, that is not the case. Communion is always available. Holy Communion. All we need to do is ask. Or touch the hand already extended.

"This is the Lamb who takes away the sins of the world; happy are those who are called to this, his eternal banquet," I began the formal prayers I say each time. Dan craned his neck to signal his willingness to receive, but then gagged at the exertion, at the slightest incline of his throat, laced as it was with sores and thick with mucus. I stopped. His mother stood beside him with a cup of water, but with his eyes he told her no. He again tried to rise up in the bed, but again he gagged.

Without saying a word, his mother sat down beside him. She gently put her arm behind him and slowly, ever so slowly tried to lift him upright. His spindly arms straightened, his trembling hands pressed against the sheets. It was no use. He coughed again, no more than a weak, phlegmy exhale. His frail chest sunk within his hospital gown. His mother slid still further onto the bed until her body was behind him, sustaining him. Her arm moved across his chest to steady him so he would not collapse forward.

It was clear Dan wanted the dignity of sitting up as best he could to offer his part of this union.

I took the tiniest sliver of the host and put it in his mouth. I could feel the heat from deep in his body, a blast from hell, of this horrid plague. He swallowed tentatively, unsure if his throat would accept or rebel. Yes, it was going down. I gave the remainder to his mother. She bowed her head in reverence just for a moment, then clutched her son all the tighter, her own tiny arms dwarfing his, no more than sticks, ravaged by the disease.

The room was so still now. I stepped toward the door. I looked back. I had stood in St. Peter's Basilica in Rome before Michelangelo's magnificent Cararra-marble rendering of that grieving mother and son. There is such profound sorrow in Mary's face. The limp body of her beloved rests in her arms, slain by the evils of that day. This was another Pietà, equally as compelling, a Pietà for anyone to readily see. The evils of another day had taken their toll. Another mother lovingly cradled her beloved son as God held both of them tenderly, wanting them to know that in the midst of their agony holy Communion was theirs.

I closed the door softly and stood in the hallway. What a privilege was mine, to share those moments, to see the magnificence of human love, of divine love.

Mother and Child

Each Thursday morning, after a quick stop at the front desk to say hello to Anne, then another stop in the chapel to focus on why I am here in the hospital, I take the elevator to the ninth floor and work my way down, usually seeing patients on each floor. I especially look forward to my stops on the second and third floors, as these promise to be happier visits, for these are the maternity floors. With stays in modern hospitals being so expensive, new mothers are usually gone the day after they give birth, so most of the babies I have the privilege of seeing are still within their first twenty-four hours of life. Their mothers may be exhausted, but their faces radiate a transcendent bliss that wipes away whatever trauma they experienced in childbirth or the fatigue left in its aftermath.

I knew something was wrong, dreadfully wrong, when I walked into the silence of Room 337 and took in Meghan, her mother, and the new baby. I have visited with parents and grandparents of newborns who are sick, but that wasn't the case here. The baby lying at Meghan's elbow was a robustly healthy little girl if I ever saw one: rosy cheeks, swaddled in pink, peacefully sleeping. I don't often cry at the sight of even the most ravenous cancer or debilitating diabetes, but day-old babies completely undo and unglue me. I can't resist touching their soft cheeks, skin so pure, so delicate, so incredibly soft as it will never again be in their lives. I can't resist burbling on to the baby and congratulating the mother.

I soon discovered that all my past words and experience were of no use, and I would have to find words I had never had to speak or even imagine before.

That silence was the first sign, the stony look on Meghan's mother's face the second. The vacant gaze on the young mother's face, the third, a look of loss at a time when she should otherwise be so happy. I would soon find out that the hours Meghan would spend with her still-unnamed baby daughter were limited. The baby, born out of wedlock, the father no longer part of Meghan's life, was to be adopted. Meghan would leave the hospital alone. About the same time, the baby would leave with her new—and overjoyed, I was sure—parents.

Who knows the circumstances of this conception and this girl's life to this point? Meghan was not yet twenty, I estimated, probably younger. The father of this child was now but a shadow in her past, this beautiful baby a reminder of what might have been. Morality, right actions and wrong, seemed but dim and useless markers for this young woman at this turning point. She was still a mother. She had felt that baby stir in her so many months before. She had felt contractions. She had pushed and gritted her teeth and pushed some more. She had looked down to see a slimy, bloody, beautiful baby held in the air, umbilical cord still joined to her.

I hadn't asked about the baby's future. Meghan's mother had volunteered the information almost as soon as I announced myself and said I was there to give them holy Communion. She announced that the baby would be adopted—and I only thought about this later—in a tone that was at once bitter and necessary. She was angry with her daughter, there was no doubt, but being a protective mother herself, she was steeling her for the separation that would soon come.

The Catholic Church believes in the physical, the tactile. That is why we apply ashes to foreheads on Ash Wednesday, why our Stations of the Cross depict in almost painful detail the events surrounding the death of Christ. It is why we have processions, why pilgrims will make their way to a holy site on their knees. The Church understood that we need visible signs, objects, and expressions to represent deeper realities, realities that cannot be expressed in words alone. Over the years, I have come to treasure these outward expressions of inner meaning. Called *sacramentals*, they—in proper theological parlance—"signify effects." In other words, they can help us to experience the touch of the divine that we need at certain moments in our lives.

I reached into the black pouch at my waist, to a larger compartment behind that which holds the hosts. I held the tiny, white plastic statue in the palm of my hand. It was my usual gift to a new mother, a statue of the Infant of Prague, the infant Christ Child who protects the young. I would customarily tell the mother to put it on a bedside table near her child so when the child's eyes first opened, he or she would see Christ and that, in turn, Christ would be watching over him or her.

Although my parish priest blessed the statues en masse, I always pronounced my own blessing over each one, assigning this particular Infant of Prague to watch over this particular infant. I looked at Meghan, so downcast and listless, her stone-faced mother and this beautiful child, took a deep breath, offered my own silent prayer for guidance, and began. "In the name of the Father, and of the Son, and of the Holy Spirit, Amen." The child stirred ever so slightly, and then the rhythmic breathing took hold once more.

"Darling child, may Christ keep you safe in the days ahead on whatever path you take, wherever you are. Always listen for his voice, because he will be speaking to you in every situation of your life. Sometimes he will be hard to hear, his voice will be so soft. But it will be there; always it will be there to guide you on the right path."

I looked up at this young mother, her eyes fixed on the smooth white sheet, her cheeks pale and dry, her face no platform for emotion. Any emotion now unleashed could so easily spin out of control, breaking down the resolve she was struggling to hold onto, a psychic cyclone that would destroy anything, everything in its path.

"Darling girl, your mother loved you so much to carry you in her body for nine months. She knows you better than anyone will ever know you, because you and she are one, never ever to be parted because this is a bond no one can break. She loves you more than you will ever know."

Meghan raised her head slowly. Our eyes met. "You did the right thing." I took in her mother now for the next words, "Meghan, you are a good girl, a good woman, and God is so proud of you. Always know that. You had other choices. You could have said no to this life that we see here this morning. But you just knew you couldn't do that. You wanted your daughter to be born. And you wanted only what was best for her. And you made a very difficult decision. You could have been selfish and held onto her, but you cared about her more than you cared about yourself."

I reached across the bed, pressed the statue into Meghan's hand, and wrapped her fingers around it.

"Your daughter will never be far from you, Meghan. Every time you look at this little statue, your daughter is going to feel, somehow, some way, that the good mother who gave her life is thinking about her, sending her love to her. When you touch this statue, she will feel that touch. It might be just when she needs it the most; you'll be right there."

I took two hosts from the pyx. "This is the Lamb of God who takes away the sins of the world, happy are those who are called to this, his eternal banquet," I pronounced the prayer. I gave one host to her, the other to her mother.

There were soft voices in the hallway outside, one nurse asking another about the proper dosage of a medication. Inside Room 337 all was quiet, but now it seemed a different quiet from when I had entered. This was not the quiet of resentment and acrimony, but the quiet of understanding—a least a fragment of understanding—and peace, if only for a time. Their heads were bowed as I left the room. Not at all bowed in shame, but touched and warmed by the presence of God in their midst.

Illness and Fairness

When illness strikes or injury occurs, most of us want to learn quickly what is wrong and how it can be remedied. In our quiet moments we also may ponder: Why did this happen to me, and what does it mean? We might search back into family medical history for an answer. The more superstitious among us peer at the tea leaves of our lives to discern what it was we once did that triggered this aneurysm or kidney malfunction, cancer or fractured arm, as if God were at the keyboard of a great computer meting out well-earned punishments for past offenses. And the question we all pose: Is it "fair" that this happened to us? To our loved ones? What is the meaning—if there is any meaning—in all of this?

If there is any place on earth where fairness or unfairness means nothing, it is surely the hospital. Cells mutating so peacefully suddenly went awry; we tripped on a carpet; we made a left turn in front of an eighteen-wheeler. Sometimes it seems that the worst among us live to be ninety-plus, with never a sick day and that the best are dealt a terrible disease that will end their life all too early. It is a mystery, and one that I have no ability to plumb. In my hospital rounds, I listen to all the reasoning and rationalizations and, knowing no way to address them, simply relate what I know to be true. The God that I know is not an unappeasable, punishing deity. God is always with us, but even more intensely—much like a solicitous parent—when we are ill. God did not land us in the hospital in order to prove something. God always stands ready to bear pain and uncertainty with us and bring us healing of mind and spirit—and if possible, body.

While God does not arbitrarily inflict injury, pain, or disease, I do believe that—if we only allow it—God always will help us find roses among the brambles, grace in the midst of difficulty. I am fairly simple-minded about this: What kind of heavenly Father would God be unless he not only soothed us, but helped us see the rays of light and promise that penetrate what we might only perceive as gloom?

Usually, as nonfatal illness and injury are assessed and treated, patients can see the physical and medical cause and effect in a clearer light. They spend their days in the hospital and go home to continue their lives. Fair or unfair, that chapter is over. And quickly put behind. They certainly put God center stage and pray fervently during their hospital stay. But with improving health and lessening need for divine help, all of us tend to go about our lives, once again relegating God to a more minor role.

When a patient faces a fatal disease, or family members face conditions that will dramatically and permanently alter their lives, a seismic shock sets off waves that reverberate in many different ways. For illness is not visited on some uniform, universal terrain, but on one textured with the unique circumstances and backdrop of those lives.

Sometimes, there is bargaining with God, either by patients or their families. Their prayers, novenas, and promises will forge a deal. Or there is denial. This too will pass, we delude ourselves, if we just don't think about it. Or a sense of immobilizing hopelessness falls like a pall, the gravity of the situation paralyzing any attempt to find a deeper meaning or redemption in an admittedly terrible situation. Honestly, who can't identify with all of these emotions?

Then, there is another emotion that illness can often invoke, as logical as it is corrosive. I began to note it more and more as I continued to make my hospital rounds.

That emotion is anger. At times anger is elevated to blind rage at the unfairness of it all. And who can blame anyone for feeling this way? Reflecting back to the life of Christ, to the Old Testament prophets, did they not fume at what had been planted in their path, holy, good, and righteous as they were? Did they deserve this kind of treatment? Did Anna in Room 532? Did Lee, who stood at the bedside of her husband in 714? Anna had been diagnosed with a fatal cancer, and Lee's husband had been admitted with a treatable initial diagnosis of fluid on the brain, which had turned out to be something far more serious and life changing.

Anna was sitting up in her bed when I entered. It was shortly after 7 AM. Her makeup was perfectly applied, nails perfectly manicured, the items on her bedside table perfectly arranged, her sheets perfectly smoothed before her. She slowly passed a rosary between her fingers, obviously praying even as we talked. Without my asking, she told me the extent of her cancer, how long she was expected to live, how she had put her worldly affairs in order and was at peace that she would soon die. Her faith sustained her. Heaven awaited her after the years of this rutted, rocky, uphill road called life on earth. Her prelude, seemingly revelatory, was ending. There was more, much more, to come.

Anna had detailed the cancer clinically, a textbook presentation of someone else. But when she began to speak about how others were treating *this* someone, her voice went up an octave, her face visibly darkened. Her husband had left her many years before, but the wound was still fresh. When he heard about her illness, he made a perfunctory phone call, nothing more. Her children didn't come to visit—or at least not often enough for her. Her jobs—to my mind, substantial—had never fulfilled her. Although she had been a conscientious employee and dutiful mother, she had been rewarded for neither, she said. That was their problem; no one had ever known her true worth. But all that was irrelevant, especially now, she maintained, sitting upright in the bed. "I have my faith," she said, clutching the rosary so tightly her knuckles were white. "Thank God I have my faith."

I looked down at her as her hand loosened on the rosary, and the beads resumed their slow, circular pattern. I didn't know what to say. It is not a faith that I could easily understand.

I stood there, pyx in hand, as Anna repeated the litany of grievances, as if I had not heard, or as if by repetition somehow the guilty parties would be notified. After a while, I took out a host, holding it in the air between us. She stopped and stared at me. "Lord, you are present in the room with us today," I began. "Let this be a good and restful day for Anna. Let her feel Christ's warm and loving presence as she takes the host, permeating her body with his holiness, and that she would know that he stands by her bed all day long. At any time, all she needs to do is reach out her own hand. His hand is already there." I placed the host on her tongue and stood back, my head bowed.

"Anna, he's with you now," I said softly. "If there is anything at all, you can let him carry it. He loves you. He wants your happiness. He wants you to know that you can rest in him and there is nothing to fear."

"I'm not afraid of anything," she countered defiantly. "But they should only know what they're doing to me, what they have done to me, what they. ..."

I hesitated at the door, smiled, albeit weakly, and waved back to her. She smoothed the sheet and took hold of the rosary with both hands. It was as if I were not there.

Anna is angry with everyone. Underneath, is she not also angry with God? A God that allowed this? Is anger a wall that keeps her from a comforting, loving relationship with God, her family, her friends? Especially at a time like this? I'm not sure, but I knew enough from my many visits to hospital rooms that anger stands in the way of healing: both physical and spiritual healing.

Anna's faith seems to be a brittle, small-print pact with a hateful God who never allows anything to happen the way we might want and always frustrates us whenever we have even the least chance of being happy on earth. It is a faith that grasps at an unreachable God in heaven, a God who will not deign to walk with us on earth and share our burdens. A God who believes we must suffer in a vale of tears so that we might better appreciate the paradise that awaits us. It is a faith that offers obeisance to an unappeasable God of exactitude, the eye of the needle being so narrow that, rich or poor, we'd best navigate carefully and only then have the slightest chance of reaching God.

I stood in the hallway for a moment. I looked at the closed door on Room 532. I wanted to go back into the room. I wanted to tell her that cancer is horrible and unfair, but God would reach her in ways she had never before experienced. That she could be a source of grace to her children, to her friends. That I had seen this happen so many times. I wanted to somehow tell her that these could be, in some ways, the best days of her life. She was free of so many of the incidentals we take so seriously. She would see herself so clearly in the days ahead. God would come to her vividly, dramatically, in breathtaking flashes.

But I didn't. Anna's wall stood before me. I was not brave enough, not enough of a man of faith to climb over it.

In Room 714, I found Lee and her husband, Charlie. He seemed a happy enough fellow, joking about his memory loss soon after I walked into the room: "It's wonderful; I can forget anything—and usually do." He wore a sleepy grin. A bandage on his head marked the spot of the exploratory surgery, but his thick, curly hair seemed determined to subsume the gauze, a follicle jungle reclaiming its territory.

He dozed off as the pain medication took effect. I turned to Lee. "I want my life back," she said starkly.

Lee had prayed and felt her prayers were answered when the neurosurgeon told her that fluid on the brain was not serious and could be treated. Then came the crushing news. Charlie's memory loss was an indication of the early stages of dementia. Although he was only in his mid fifties, Charlie would continue to deteriorate mentally. He would gradually lose the ability to feed and wash himself. He would be bedridden.

"We had such a good life," Lee said as she began to cry. "Now I'm going to have to do everything for him. Look, I love this guy, but this is more than I want. Why, why did this happen to us? I prayed, I prayed so hard."

I gently told Lee that God would hear her prayers, and she would have a life. But it would not be the same life. No, it wasn't fair. But in God's mysterious plan for her life there was to be meaning in Charlie's illness for her. Even as I spoke those words, other patients I had known were flashing across my mind, little cameos of people heartsick at devastating news like this, and yet who found a new power, a new meaning in their lives as they or loved ones faced challenges that seemed impossible to withstand.

I held Lee's hand and prayed. "Lord Jesus Christ, we know so little about your ways. And yet, as we look back over our lives, we see that you were always there, even when you seemed so distant, and we felt abandoned. The worst of times opened us to the best of times. Let Lee know that you are here now. That you will be with her in ways we cannot see right now, but she will know in the days ahead. There will be difficult moments, to be sure. But every now and then, she will just know that you have touched her, that she has seen your face. In the face of Charlie, in the faces of those who will comfort and help her. Known people, total strangers. We place ourselves in your loving hands, knowing that you who made us care for us so. Lord, we're going to wake Charlie now, and Lee and Charlie are going to receive this magnificent gift, the Eucharist."

She touched Charlie's cheek and his eyes blinked open. "You are together today," I said. "You will be together in the days ahead. Together in the strength and peace of God."

A smile flickered across Charlie's face. He chewed two times and swallowed. His eyes closed. Lee looked over at him, then at me. I could tell she was holding onto the Eucharist and had not yet swallowed. She pulled up the sheets to cover her husband's shoulders and patted him gently on the cheek.

John's Birthday

While my assigned mission at the hospital is to take holy Communion to Catholic patients, just walking these hallways over the past dozen or so years has provided a passport into so many other lives. I am not a staff member, therefore in a hurry. I am not a patient, likely with needs. I am not a visitor, seeking assurance or more information about the status of a loved one.

I believe that this entrée into the lives of an incredibly wide and diverse range of people—many of whom I see each week—has everything to do with the contents of that black pouch. God is present in those consecrated hosts. Something beyond our understanding that ever so subtly connects within people, signaling that they can unburden themselves or simply have a moment of rest or comfort or reassurance within a busy day? That they can relax their professional selves for a moment and touch the God of us all, who does not call us Catholic or Protestant, Jew or Muslim—or atheist, for that matter—but looks upon us all as God's children, all beloved. A solicitous God who wants to be with us in the circumstances we find ourselves in at that very moment.

There are the intensive care nurses, like Grace (oh, to have Grace at your bedside, not only watching the monitors, but lovingly stroking your hair) and Anna (her richly hued skin and soft, slightly accented voice such a soothing balm in this place of beeps and blinking lights). I'm careful not to interfere with their work, so I always ask if they have time to receive. If I see that they are involved in a procedure, I just nod and move on.

I usually catch Grace on her travels between cubicles, so we can stand beside the sink in the cardiac ICU "bullpen" at the center of the unit as I offer a prayer for her strength and astuteness in her work. "Grace, your patients can't see God's face, but they see your face. They can't feel God's hands, but they feel your hands. You are his face, his hands today. He will be with you when things get harried, when you feel you just can't go on. That's when you will know he is with you, all the more. He comes to us when we need him most. This is the Lamb of God." I pronounce the eucharistic prayer and give her the host. Eyes closed, her customary, audible exhale tells me that God has entered, and fatigue and anxiety have been swept away.

One morning when I saw Anna, whom I had not seen for a few weeks, she not only had time for the Eucharist but also wanted to tell me about how her family had gathered for her father's funeral. We often exchanged a word or two, but it was obvious this time she wanted to share her experience before receiving Communion.

Her family were migrant workers from the Rio Grande, she began, traveling the circuit south to north, following the crops each year, eight children in all. To look at this beautiful and competent woman, who would have ever pictured her bent over a row of celery in Texas or on a ladder in Utah plucking cherries from a tree? But here we were, in the midst of a busy intensive care unit, talking about the values her father had instilled in his children. How his sternness masked his knowledge of the uphill road ahead. How his insistence on their education bore another kind of rich harvest: All eight children went on to higher education and professional careers.

"I never knew summer was vacation time," she said, smiling. "We went on the road in April and got back in September, usually after school had started. But miss a day? Not on your life."

We offered the Eucharist in memory of this newest saint in heaven, a man who now could rest from so many years of the hardest labor.

Another hospital friend is Jim, a cardiologist. He talks about a great lesson in his religion class, which he admits, again sheepishly, he doesn't attend often enough, and segues into talking about his son in high school, the family trip to Europe, and his busy practice, which he speaks about with a quality I see often enough in physicians. "Jim, you love what you do, don't you?" to which he replies, beaming as if it is the first time he has been asked and has had an answer ready for the thirty years he's been in practice, "And I feel so lucky, so darned lucky to do it."

And Brian, a pulmonologist, whom I see all too often in the ICU, as he uses his considerable skills to coax old or diseased lungs into providing air for his patients to survive, and hopefully, thrive. His deep Jewish faith, bestowed by parents who loved and kept alive the tradition and rituals, is at a standstill. His reasons are many: a busy life as a doctor, a Christian wife who is indifferent to religion, the small Jewish community in our city, growing children who hear the siren call of popular culture much louder than the ram's horn of the ancients. But the hunger is there within Brian; I know because he brings up something about faith or belief each time I see his smiling, youthful face. There are no great breakthroughs in our short visits at the hospital, but I feel he knows that when he sees me in the hall, he can at least remind himself that our God awaits him when the time is right.

Steve is an internist and an end-of-life specialist. Few of his patients have any other than the grimmest outlook; many will only leave the hospital on the mortician's gurney. He took a moment one week to receive the Eucharist after an hour-long session with family members, urging them in the gentlest of ways—he reminds me of Jimmy Stewart, complete with shy, mumbled words—to allow their mother to pass on. After he received the Eucharist, he would be signing an order that dialysis be stopped. "Lord, that you would be with that family and let them know you await their loving mother," I prayed with him. "And let Steve know that his love and concern for that family makes all the difference in the world and makes this difficult decision so much easier for them."

Every so often a nurse or student nurse is in the room as I give the patient the Eucharist, and either they will say they are Catholic, or they will make the Sign of the Cross. To give them both the Eucharist unites them in Christ. Spiritually, this is certainly a propitious moment; emotionally it brings them together in a way beyond telling. I treasure those moments when the healer and the one in need of healing of the living God.

From time to time, just because I'm at the hospital and people know I am Catholic, I can help with some of the thornier temporal issues of this wonderful, but sometimes legalistic, Church of mine.

Anne, a volunteer answering the phone at the front desk, took me aside one day and said she was dating this "really nice guy" whom she first knew in the third grade in New York and now has gotten back in touch with. She wanted to obtain an annulment for her Catholic marriage that had only lasted a few years and was now decades behind her, but she was leery. She had heard horror stories of other divorced women for whom the process was humiliating and painful. I made a few phone calls and found the right, sympathetic person at the diocesan tribunal and was able to give Anne the phone number that would lead to not only the annulment, but eventually to her marrying that nice guy, Jack.

And then there is Bonnie, a nurse and single mom whose red hair takes on a different shade every few weeks or so, depending on the mood of her stylist. If I ask Jim the cardiologist about the state of his soul, I always ask Bonnie about the state of her love life. The latest is a man she met through the Internet and, although he lives some thousand miles away, there is a light in her eye about this one. As I give her Communion in the hallway, I pray that all goes well on the floor that day—and that Mr. Right will indeed come her way.

I knew something of her life and its heartaches. Her twenty-one-year-old son John—a friend of my own son, Noah—was killed in a motorcycle accident. He had his troubles with school and drugs, Bonnie admitted. We prayed for him in the weeks after the funeral, Bonnie softly sobbing each time. On one Thursday, Bonnie produced a picture of John astride that motorcycle. It was his birthday, the first birthday he was not with her.

At times like this I find the less I say, the better. I just stood there with her, my hand over hers on top of the chart of the patient she was about to see.

"There were a lot of heartaches with that boy," she began, "but I remember one birthday in Myrtle Beach. He was just a teenager. We just had the best time together at the beach, eating out, talking. It was just perfect. Perfect. And then—then this—" Her voice dropped off. "He always went too fast, at everything." I held her hand tighter.

"He died out there on River Road, just didn't make the turn. Too fast, too fast."

"If I told you I understood this, I'd be lying," I said. "If I tried to convince you it's 'God's plan' I hope you'd never talk to me again. Would God plan this, want this? No, not the God I know. Who can figure all this out? None of us, that's who. But that wonderful kid is looking down on us right now, Bonnie. That much I know. That much I'm sure of. We're sad, terribly sad. But he's saying, 'Mom, don't worry, I'm okay now.'"

Bonnie looked up at me. "I can just see him out there on River Road that day, breezing along, so happy. He was doing exactly what he loved to do the most. And I guess God just decided to call him right then and there." We stood in silence for a while.

I took a host from the pyx. "John, you're looking down on us right now," I began. "We both can feel it. Here's wishing you a happy birthday, and your mom wishes you were right here to celebrate it. But that's not the way it turned out. You were only twenty-one when God took you, but John, you know more about life than we do; you're there with God. And here we are, kind of muddling along. Your mom is thankful for every day she had with you, John. You know that. Now it's your turn to take care of her. Let her feel your presence, let her know it's all okay. Pass her prayers along. You're in a great place to do that."

After saying the eucharistic prayer, I put a host on Bonnie's tongue. Most people receive by accepting the host in their hands, but Bonnie was old-fashioned in this respect. She bowed her head, and when she looked up at me the tears were almost gone. A mother's love had replaced the grief in her eyes. "He was a good boy. He is a good boy," she corrected herself. "He'll always be mine, that's the wonderful part."

The Sacred and
the Ordinary

Connections

My objective—my mission, if you will—as I visit hospital rooms each week is to connect people with God. A God who is seeking them, hungering for them, awaiting them. A God I have come to know in my own life as a patient, loving friend—with an excellent sense of humor, by the way, as God follows our moral and spiritual detours—who wants to be with each of us at every moment, but especially when times are tough. After all, what is a good friend about but that?

But before I introduce this spiritual connection, I try to connect on a human level. Although I am the bearer of a gift so supreme and profound, it is not in my nature to enter a room as if Gregorian chant were wafting through incense-suffused air, gravely intone my prayers, dispense the Eucharist, and silently slip away. I try, as best I can, to actually "see" who I am talking to, and in the few minutes we have together somehow relate to one another as human beings.

These "connections" have produced fascinating interchanges and entrées into people's lives, and at least one, well, connection I could never have imagined.

If the name on my list has a familiar ethnic ring to it, that is a sure invitation. If it is a Quinn or O'Reilly, I might say as I approach the bed, "My orders were to bring Communion to any good Irishman (or Irishwoman) in the hospital today; might there be any in this room?" It may sound corny, but inevitably it brings a smile, even from the sickest of patients. They have been singled out; someone knows something about them beyond their blocked arteries, suppressed autoimmune system, or the name on their wristband.

A Slavic name might have me greeting them with a *dobré ráno*—"good morning" in my own Slovak language—and close enough to Polish and Russian to be understood. One morning this started a marvelous conversation with a man whose father worked in the same coal mines as my own father around Scranton, Pennsylvania. So, when the time came for the Eucharist to be received, I could pray for both our fathers, the hard-working men who provided for us, the strong faith that sustained them and their families in the most difficult of times. It is part of our rich and shared history: The tiny piece of bread received this day in this hospital room was received in those coalfields, received in the tiny villages of Slovakia from which those brave immigrants came, most around the turn of the twentieth century.

An accent provides still another opening. Having spent many years in and around New York City, I can almost tell whether the person with that rubbery lower jaw producing a distinctive nasal twang is from Queens, Long Island, or New Jersey. One morning, inspired,

I blurted out "Rego Park" to have the woman in the bed, recovering from a hysterectomy, simply beam. Not only a Queens, New York, accent—a Rego Park, Queens, New York, accent. If the person is from Long Island, I ask what town; if New Jersey, what exit—the defining geographical cross hairs of these two areas. I usually can forge a further connection—if Long Island, we roll our eyes together about the Long Island Expressway's ever-congested lanes. If New Jersey, something about the rebirth of Hoboken or the lower price of gas in the stations just before the tunnels into New York City.

A southern accent, one I do not hear too often, as Catholics in the South were rare and are still a bit of an endangered species here in the Bible belt, brings a look of incredulity and a comment along the lines of "Not many of you around in those days, were there?" This often leads to stories about being Catholic in a largely Protestant region, folk tales and misapprehensions of how we adore statues, blindly obey the Vatican, and for some strange reason eat only fish on Friday—or used to, anyhow.

All are avenues to the soul. When I touch on even the smallest somethings about people that individualize them, I am all the more prepared to pray with them specifically, not only about their situation or recovery, but about who they are. A New York City policeman and a Mississippi Delta pharmacist's wife are each Catholic, but their religious experience, their backgrounds, are so vastly different. To treat them the same, pray the same, talk the same, would be terribly impersonal. All have certain touchstones in their lives, and if it is possible to find them in our short time together, we create a stronger bond, and the Eucharist, that most personal of gifts, becomes that much more personal.

My hospital visits have allowed me to cross paths with people I could easily have met under other circumstances. Like the diabetic whose leg had just been amputated below the knee, who served on the USS Yellowstone, the repair ship, at the same time I served on the USS Power, one of the destroyers it tended at the Mayport, Florida, Navy base. The sprightly woman with ovarian cancer who skated with Ice Follies in the years I saw that show in Cleveland. The acknowledged alcoholic who used to drink at the White Horse, one of my Greenwich Village haunts: We may have been elbow-to-elbow late one bleary night, who knows?

This kind of chitchat might seem to have nothing to do with the Eucharist, but of course it does. We are each wayfarers on the road of life, pausing under a sheltering tree, to tell our stories before we share a meal. A meal that means so much more because we know at least something of one another.

When there was another person in the room who is the opposite sex of the patient, I used to assume and say "husband" or "wife." After enough mistakes, when the other person turned out to be a daughter, son, or "significant other," I began to refer to that person as a "loved one, here with you today." But when I have ascertained that indeed it is a husband or wife, I ask how many years they've been married and if it's been many—usually the case—I offer something like, "(number) years; never a harsh word, right? Just like my marriage." Yes, there have been the few who looked quizzically at me as if to say, "You're right, we haven't ever had a harsh word," but 99 percent of the time they look lovingly at each other, acknowledging the shared battle scars.

When I later meet these people outside the hospital, some talk about the visit and thank me, but more often than not, receiving the Eucharist at that crucial time in their lives is too intimate and immediate a moment to relive. We will usually talk about our worldly connections, the happenstance and common things that inexorably link us together. One, two, three, or no degrees of separation.

When I entered Room 536 to find Mary Ethel Mahoney, my opening was obvious. How Irish can you be? She must have been, as they say, "a fine cut of woman," with her high cheekbones and dancing eyes. Trained as a dental hygienist, she went back to work after the Mahoney children were older, but kept the application for a new job secret until the call came through. For the next twelve years, she was an aide on a school bus for handicapped children. The best job she ever had, she smiled.

Mary Ethel had lost weight as the kidney disease and dialysis ravaged her body, and it was clear she would not live much longer. I held her hand and told her of God's great love for her, and that in receiving the Eucharist God would give her the strength for these days, that she was a good and brave woman. Her husband, Ed, stood by, a handsome man in his mid seventies with a face that always wore the hint of a kindly smile. They had been married forty-five years.

Her obituary appeared a few weeks later, but it wasn't until many months later that I happened to see Ed after Mass on a Sunday morning. We exchanged greetings and talked about Mary Ethel, and that might have been the extent of our relationship. But each time I saw him after that, and it was not all that often, his kindly smile and quiet dignity at his dying wife's bedside came vividly into focus. What a good man. It was so sad that he was now alone, without his precious Mary Ethel.

About a year after her death I met an attractive, vital woman whose husband had died shortly after their moving to our city to retire. Another happy, long marriage cruelly cut short. The next step was obvious. I had Ed and the woman over for dinner. The pretense was for them to start a bereavement group for widows and widowers of my parish.

They started the group but no, the fairy-tale ending was not to be. They did not marry. The small group grew to about thirty, and they quickly decided theirs was not to be a bereavement group but a social and service club where they might go to brunch or a movie together as well as collect winter coats for the needy. Within that group was an attractive widow named Pat, who, while she was a member of our parish, may never have met Ed without it.

They're celebrating their first anniversary as of this writing, and with their combined total of six children and seventeen grandchildren have found that love is, if not lovelier, certainly lovely the second time around. Had I only given Ed and Mary Ethel Mahoney holy Communion that morning four years before and done nothing more, who knows what would have happened?

Holy Water

Her daughter met me at the hospital-room door. Through her surgical mask, she told me that Mom wasn't doing well at all. No, she wasn't; I could see that as I came closer to the bed. There was a weak smile on Mom's face, the valiant statement of a woman—who, if the lines on her face could speak—would tell of a life that had its share of heartaches. Her bright peroxide hair showed an inch-deep muddy streak of gray, the beauty parlor no longer the priority it once was as she had tried to hold back the march of time. The march that had carved rivulets in her sunken cheeks and forehead. The march that had probably not seen the best medical care. She had tried to keep the surface looking as good as she could, with what she had, even if she may not have had the means to care for the rest of herself.

I took her hand and just looked at her for a moment. The hand, so cold, so thin, rough with the years of hard work in a textile mill. I asked how she was doing, and she just shrugged her shoulders, bony even through the thick sweatshirt her daughter had brought to keep her warm. I reached out for the daughter's hand, and she in turn took her mother's other hand, and I began my prayer.

There are only a few moments to assess the situation in each room I visit. There are usually some telltale signs—the look on a person's face, the presence or lack of flowers and cards, the presence or lack of a loved one, the smell of alcohol or cigarettes, religious items, the kind of book they are reading, the clothes visitors wear. As a reporter, I have some training in sizing up people and places, but when I bring holy Communion to people I try to put pieces together in another way. What is the story of this soul? What does this person need right now? How can I help promote the healing of mind, body—and if God wills—spirit? I close my eyes and, remembering the words of Scripture that Christ told his followers not to fret, that they would know what to say and how to say it, I begin.

"Rosie, God is very close to you right now. Soon you will receive him in the Eucharist. Here is your caring daughter, looking over you with the same loving concern that you showed to her when she was just a little girl. Now she has the privilege of looking after you. God is looking after you as well, holding you right now in his arms and telling you in words that we can't hear—but you can hear, Rosie—that you need not worry. He is here now; he will be here all day and all night." I took a host from the pyx. "This is the Lamb of God who—"

I broke the host in two and gave her one half, her daughter the other. "Now, you are joined together in a way unlike any other way: mother, daughter, and God."

Rosie took a deep breath and then exhaled audibly, a sigh of recognition and relief that I often hear at that moment. She closed her eyes, shyly. I was ready to leave, but her daughter stopped me. She had another request, she said, a bit tentatively.

She went to a brown paper bag on the sill and produced a pickle jar. At the bottom were sand and a few seashells. The liquid, she told me, was ocean water. Mom loved the ocean. And if she couldn't get there right now, her daughter wanted to bring the ocean to her. She had filled the jar this morning. Her daughter knew I wasn't a priest, but she asked: Would I please bless this water?

In the years I have been making these weekly visits, I've learned to follow my instincts and that most requests can usually be met. If I say yes, the way will come to answer the need. "Yes, of course I will bless the water," I said.

I held the pickle jar in my left hand and said a prayer of blessing. The sand quickly settled. The water glistened in the morning light coming through the Venetian blinds, sending shivers of reflected light across the bed sheets. "Lord, here is the ocean that Rosie loves so much, just a glassful really, a small part of the vastness of those great waters. We are all but a glassful. Yet without each of us that ocean would be missing something. Here is Rosie and her daughter right at her side, all of us asking you to bring healing to this good woman. Let this water be a sign of your healing power, your greatness that has no limits. And how we can be lost in the vastness of your mercy.

"For just a moment, lift her up from this bed, Lord, and take her to the shore, and let her walk along in that sand and feel that ocean water swirling over her feet. At her favorite place. You know it and she knows it. Right there. And let her stand in that spot and look out to that horizon where you live and know that nothing, nothing can ever keep you apart from her. Let her feel that warmth that only you can give, that peace that nothing can harm us, nothing. Because we are yours. You are ours."

I am constantly being educated about the deepest needs in all of us, about the interplay of sacred and secular, temporal and spiritual, holy and ordinary. While it may not always be startling or apparent (our own blindness to God's graces?), people are constantly urging us to bring God into their lives, to bless them, to bless their lives, to honor those things precious to them. And as I—a layperson, father and husband, a writer by trade—have discovered in my hospital work, this is not only the venue of the ordained or the professionally religious.

Yes, the holy Eucharist is the primary and compelling reason for my visiting Rosie and yes, I believe that it is the Real Presence of Christ, of God, in our midst. But opportunities such as this allow anyone to make the simple statement that God's presence is everywhere. That we are all—if we assent—bearers of his grace. That we are the connective tissue between a sometimes distant and faceless God and the immediate needs that all of us have. That we can bless in so many different words, in so many different ways.

As I thought about it, such is the continuing, confusing, wonderful mystery of the mingling of sacred and the ordinary, of God and each of us. I certainly believe we are made holier by receiving the Eucharist. God enters us physically and spiritually, bringing God's presence to us in the most intimate and immediate way to take rest in our souls, meanwhile coursing through our cells and flowing in our bloodstream. Is this only a one-way street?

But, I thought as I stood there a while longer, might not something also happen to the immutable, unchangeable God as God comes into our world and lives each day, in us, in this way? Could it be that God is, in a way, reincarnated, reborn? God rejoins the human race, which God created and of which God was once part. God renews God's covenant. God recommits to us.

I looked down the hall. The list was long. It was time to see another patient.

A Family Affair

Sickness, just as life, doesn't only happen to an individual. Family, loved ones—those bonded by blood, affection, or mere proximity—are swept into its vortex, churned by the inconclusive and troubling test results, buoyed by remission and healthier counts, standing by as mute witnesses to the patient's changing condition and fate. The hospital room becomes the crucible where there is no escape from the past, the present is everything, and the future, well, the future will come another day, to be dealt with on its own terms.

That is why I have tried, over these years at the hospital, to include everyone in the room when I say my spontaneous prayers and, at times, initiate an impromptu ritual. I am always mindful of the singularity of my purpose, but I do not believe that a "one size fits all" approach, or merely the proper recitation of the prescribed words, is sufficient. Each situation demands its own response, hopefully one that is sensitive and mindful of how this might help not only the patient in the bed, but also the others in the room. When it comes to families, I try as best I can to "see" their dynamics and adapt my visit to their rhythms and signals, building upon a strong family foundation or mending the ties of those broken.

It is usually not difficult to assess a family's profile when entering a room. If a son or daughter is off to the side, saying little or nothing, ready to bolt at a hint of conversation about the state of the body or soul of the person in the bed, or anything even vaguely religious or spiritual, it's a signal that this could easily be the first time these family members have been together in years, drawn together by a sudden, serious illness, the imminence of death.

I do the best I can to bring the alienated son or daughter back, and sometimes I succeed. In the best of times, they look down sheepishly and assent. In less than the best of times, they will not allow God to thaw that icy shield that has separated them from themselves, their God, their family.

So it was one morning as I stood beside the bed of a woman who had tubes draining a bloody liquid from her body. Her son stood near the window. He would not make eye contact even when I spoke to him. His longish hair was unruly and unwashed, his jeans filthy. He was in his mid to late thirties, past the age where this might be a sign of youthful abandonment or rebellion. No, he shook his head; he did not want to receive Communion. I began my prayer.

"Lord, on this beautiful summer's day, you shine into this room; we feel your grace, your presence. You, the Son of God, right here with us, right now. How wonderful you are, and we are grateful for your presence. And here, we have the presence of a wonderful son who has come to be with his beloved mother. She always answered his call when he was growing up; she was always there. Now, he has come to her aid because he loves her so much. Bless them both, Lord, throughout this day and in the days ahead. Bring your healing power to this good woman that she might soon be back home. And to her good son. Amen."

I took a host from the pyx and held it in the air as I said the eucharistic prayer. His downcast eyes slowly flickered upward, and for just an instant, we looked at each other. There was such sadness, such profound sadness in those eyes. I took the host and, consciously, I carried that sadness—whatever it represented—to his mother. She would want him healed. She knew what lay behind those sad eyes. Although she was the patient, he also was in pain. She needed to take the Son of God to herself as well as her own son. His healing would hasten her healing.

Or, if it is like what I encountered in Room 548 on one of the Thursdays in Lent, with four grown children clustered about the bed, the family picture is different and clear. At the mention of why I am there, they smile and look expectantly to their eighty-year-old mother, repeating what I have just said. She lay in bed. Her wig is a little off to the side, her eyes closed, her skin ashen from radiation and chemotherapy, but her tiny smile and nod indicated she wanted to assure her children she's heard and appreciated their concern. She had almost died the day before, her oncologist told me. But here she was, alive to see another day and gaze upon her own.

These family moments, not gathered around a happy Thanksgiving table laden with food, or in a living room wading through a sea of Christmas wrapping paper, but around a hospital bed, are sacramental themselves. They are family, and a family who shares Christ together is together. In him, with each other.

I found that these were but four of the seventeen children that Cathy had borne. Dozens of grandchildren: a sprawling, contentious, elastic, and ultimately loving family. They told me stories of broken bones and Mom catching them with a contraband bottle of vodka on prom night, the clothesline hung with diapers, and diapers, and diapers, for years, and years, and years. Then it was time for the other sacrament for this sacramental moment.

I took five hosts from the pyx and held them in the palm of my hand. "Dear Lord, you have blessed this good woman with children so abundantly—maybe even more abundantly than she and her beloved Hal, who is there with you in heaven, looking down on us, might have planned for." They chuckled and Mom opened her eyes to reveal a knowing grin. "Here they are, representing all seventeen of her children. As she lovingly tended to them, stood by their bedside when they needed her, they are here, with mom, right at her bedside, with so much love.

"Now, this family is going to be joined together in one another, and in a very special way. In you. The God of the Ages, the God slow to anger and rich in mercy. Bring your choicest blessings upon this good woman; let it be a peaceful, restful day for her. Speak to her in the soft voice of your comforting love. Hold her; shelter her under your mighty wings this day. And bless each of them, bless their brothers and sisters, their children, all of them here in spirit today."

I gathered the hosts into a small stack and gently placed one host on her tongue, the others in the outstretched hands of her children.

One of her daughters held a straw and cup to her mother's dry mouth. She swallowed and lay back on the pillow, her vein-encrusted hands resting comfortably on her stomach, the fingers gnarled with age, her well-worn wedding band dangling about her ring finger, just a bony shadow of what it once was. Her eyes were closed. If there is such a facial expression as a holy smile, Cathy was wearing it.

I believe that the Eucharist is a wellspring of grace, grace that gives strength to bear one's own pain or that of a loved one. I believe that God-given grace radiates exponentially into each life as a person takes the Body of Christ, in this, the deepest way in which we are able to experience God during our earthly life.

The Last Supper, when the Eucharist began, was a meal. A group of ragtag, mostly uneducated followers gathered around a man who had dazzled and frightened them. They witnessed sublime moments and they fought among themselves. They were at turns heroic believers in his message and pitifully weak doubters. The Scriptures do not paint a picture-perfect portrait. They had sinned. They would sin again. He broke the unleavened bread, looked up to heaven, asked God's blessing upon it, and passed to all those at the table. Even to the one who would, in a matter of a few hours, betray him.

Worthy or Not

Magie Noire!

Attraction!

Ô Oui!

One after another, the perfumes rose up to tantalize me with their promise. The spell each cast with but a drop of its essence made me dizzy. Seduction…desire…soft music…silk sheets…love. Ah, the allure of it all. Praise God for the olfactory system. There I was at the Lancôme counter at an upscale department store in my city, searching for the perfect Mother's Day present for my wife, Tracy, my hands bristling with tiny slivers of paper, each bearing its distinctive scent.

That's when I noticed a woman at the neighboring counter, the distinctive Chanel logo on her smock, staring intently at me through well-etched eyes. She began to smile, not a commercial smile, something much warmer. The look on her face signaled she knew me. She began to speak.

"Are you a priest?"

"No, I'm not," I said.

"I remember you," she began hesitantly. "I remember when you came into my baby's room," she continued. "The helicopter was already on the pad ready to take him up to Duke Medical Center. He was sick, so sick. We thought he was going to die. I don't know your name, but I'll never forget that moment. You touched him so tenderly and blessed his tiny forehead. You gave me holy Communion, and you said the most beautiful prayer I've ever heard. You said God would be on that helicopter with my son. And then they whisked us out of there. I don't know if that's all you said, but you brought a sense of calm in what must not have taken more than a couple seconds. I felt a sense of peace come over me. I did feel God was with us and I knew," and here she hesitated, collecting herself, "I just knew from that moment on that he was going to be all right. He's now a rambunctious six-year-old, and I just want to say," her clouded eyes wrinkled into a mother's proud grin, "thank you."

I stood there speechless. How strange, mysterious, and fortunate is this life of ours.

I was privileged to be with that woman and her ill son in a room six years before, bringing the Lamb of God, the Eucharist, to her in that hour of profound need, because two simple words were written into a Church document that few Catholics have ever read.

One of the truly dramatic changes in modern Catholic life was set in motion with the repetition, four times, of the words, "active participation." They appeared in the first constitution to be issued by the Second Vatican Council. Although the assembled bishops, archbishops, and cardinals of the Church would hesitate and wrestle over many other issues before, during, and after the four council sessions between 1962 and 1965, they were apparently both eager to speak and unified in spirit in the 1963 document *Sacrosanctum Concilium,* the Constitution on the Sacred Liturgy. "The people of God," who were members of the "priesthood of all believers" (as later Vatican II documents would triumphantly enfranchise all Catholics), were no longer to be a passive audience in the Mass but partners in raising up to God in song, word, and action in this, the very cornerstone of Catholic worship. The days of a priest intoning Latin words with his back to the silent faithful, were soon to be over. And with the changes *Sacrosanctum Concilium* set in motion came an opportunity that dramatically affected my life.

If few at the time read the Second Vatican Council documents, fewer still understood their practical impact. In April 1969, the Sacred Congregation for the Discipline of the Sacraments' instruction *Fidei Custos* (On Special Ministers to Administer Communion) performed an adroit literary and ecclesial two-step to both maintain Church consistency and put the council's wishes into effect:

> *As guardian of the faith, the Church carefully preserves the deposit of that faith unchanged through the ages. But when special circumstances and new demands arise, the Church changes prudently and at the same time magnanimously the purely canonical norms it has legislated.*

The Sacred Congregation designated "special ministers [who] may give communion to themselves and to the faithful." They were to be

chosen in this order of preference: subdeacons, clerics in minor
orders, those who have received tonsure, men religious, women
religious, male catechists (unless, in the prudent judgment of
the pastor, a male catechist is preferable to a woman religious),
laymen, laywomen.

With this quaintly chauvinistic document, a dam had burst. Although I came in second to last, I still made the list.

I had grown up in a Catholic Church where no one but the priest could touch the consecrated host, where strict admonitions by the Notre Dame Sisters warned me not to bite or chew the host, once received on my outstretched tongue. I was to reverently let it dissolve in my mouth, usually dry, as a strict fast from eating or drinking after midnight was mandatory.

An announcement of a special sale item over the public address system brought me back from a Vatican document to the floor of an American department store. I looked at this beautiful, tearful woman standing before me as customers streamed by. I was numb, dumb. But my mind was racing.

How fortunate we both were to have this precious gift of God in our lives in this real, tactile, and magnificently powerful way. How fortunate that we met, although under circumstances neither of us would have asked for, and now are bonded in a way so deep and lasting. She does not know my name. I do not know hers or her son's. But all that surface knowledge is irrelevant in the face of a relationship that weaves like a winding country road, through our lives, through God, and back to us again.

How fortunate that those assembled bishops opened wide the

gates of grace for the many more who would be able to receive the Body of Christ in hospitals and homes and for those who would bring it to them. Unworthy as some of us are, myself for certain, we are all equal in this commission, performing as the priesthood not of a few, elevated, but in a common priesthood with Christ, radiating from his time on earth to this very moment.

I reached out and embraced her. We said nothing; there was nothing more to say. Everything was going to be all right.

Among the
Unworthy

The Hidden Sickness

Fear. Sheer terror. Excruciating pain. These are common currency in the hospital, the more obvious and readily understandable mental and biological shackles of our minds and bodies. For too many of the people I see on my Thursday rounds there is another sickness—a hidden sickness—that is even more physically debilitating and spiritually corrosive.

I learned to spot it early in my years of hospital visits. "Well, I went to Catholic school," followed by a long pause, is a sure, diagnostic giveaway. "I haven't been practicing all—all that much," with an accompanying stammer, is another. "You see, my wife is a (fill in the denomination), and I married outside the Church," underscored with an embarrassed look, is a giveaway of what is to follow. And then, the textbook phrase: "I haven't led the best life; I'm not really worthy."

What are these pitiable words coming from people recovering from assaults to their bodies through surgery or with their body chemistry awry with a flood of albumin or potassium? How could people most in need of God wall themselves off from God's presence? It is because of the hidden illness, seemingly transmitted in the DNA of Catholics as no other Christian faith can claim.

Guilt. The illness is guilt. Irrational, unfounded, unbridled guilt.

It is a rare Thursday that I do not find a guilty Catholic or two—or even three or four—believing they are condemned to suffer alone, without God's healing power in the Eucharist. They are locked in an eternal, Sisyphean battle within themselves, and, while an inner voice softly whispers they should not keep God at arm's length, a chorus of still other voices from a distant past thunder, "Guilty as charged."

So it was with Jane on a grim, cold January day in the Carolinas. Her hair, patchy and unruly, a swirl of different colors and textures, had grown back after the first round of chemotherapy. A lone saline-solution bag hung on the pole beside her bed, so it wasn't immediately evident how she was doing. As we talked, it was soon clear: colon cancer, stage four. Further treatment would be suspended. And so, when I offered to give her holy Communion, and she looked down, murmuring that she could not, I asked why.

"It's just the way I was raised," she said. She admitted that she hadn't been to confession in many years. And then, the real reason: Suddenly, on that damp January morning, we were sent back to other damp and sad mornings spent in a first grade classroom in her native England.

"It was a Catholic school," she began in a quiet voice, with only the slightest tinge of a British accent. "On Mondays, sister would ask those of us who hadn't been to Mass on Sunday to raise our hands. I was only six years old; lying wasn't in my nature. So, I raised my hand. Those of us who had raised our hands were ushered outside the room to be caned. I came back into the room, trying so hard not to cry, but it hurt. Inside and out."

"I did that a few more times and was caned each time. Then it dawned on me. When the Monday morning question was asked, I kept my hand down. I lied. That was my first impression of the Church, of God punishing me because my parents hadn't taken me to Church. That I was bad. In fact, I deserved to be beaten with that cane."

I looked down at this good and honest woman in her chair beside the bed. She said, "Yes, I would love to receive. I was just at a friend's funeral at St. Mark's, and I so wanted to go up for Communion. I just couldn't. I can't."

I took the pyx from the leather pouch and opened it. That morning, as usual, I had gone to the small chapel within our parish school annex for the hosts. As I took the cover off the ciborium, I looked down to see a strange sight. This time, instead of dozens of the usual, neat, round pieces, there were many oddly misshaped pieces, the remnants of a huge host consecrated at one of the daily Masses.

I paused in that quiet, airless room. A flickering flame from the vigil lamp played on the side of the tabernacle. I stared down into the cup. My mind wandered.

Christ's body, broken for us.

How could he, who suffered so much to show that God understood what it was to be human, and that his love transcended anything we might do, forget us and our needs? How could he turn away after joining himself so intimately with us the created, not through some dramatic and fantastical act, but in the ordinariness of daily life, willingly sharing in our pain? How could he, who forgave those who killed him, not forgive us? I looked at those jagged edges, those tiny squares and rectangles, that were in one practical sense the result of the scoring on the back of the host, invisible to the congregation, that made it easier for the celebrant to crack the host apart for distribution. In another sense, a God of many sizes and shapes who conforms to us.

Even before I had read them, I always liked the idea behind the two classics written by Abraham Joshua Heschel, a great Jewish thinker, social activist, and mystic who was sometimes criticized within Judaism because his expansive religious beliefs were not intellectually, dogmatically, and historically rigorous enough. He saw the spiritual life from two points of view. Another of his books, *Man is Not Alone*, conveys an understandable-enough approach. But my favorite has always been *God in Search of Man*.

When I find the reluctant or the guilty on my rounds, I don't ask them to make some categorical declaration of their intent. Intent will develop as we talk—or it will not—and I will know. I simply go on, feeling that they will stop me—if they indeed do want me to stop. Grace knows no bounds; God is the God of unbound mercy. We are the ones who limit what God can do and be in our lives.

Yes, the Church offers the sacrament of reconciliation, a wonderful, healing gift. The people I visit are sick, often confused, frightened. Can I stand before them and forgive their sins? I am not a priest; I cannot hear their confession. I can offer to have a priest visit, but this moment also asks for something.

All of us want forgiveness, for another person to know us, to know what we have been through, how life has treated us, how we have responded, well or not. And then to accept us. By listening and taking on whatever it is that burdens them, we do accept them and lighten that heavy load. So while I cannot forgive in the formal sacramental sense, I can be with Jane in another way: two frail human beings standing humbly before God.

I prayed that together we could rise from self-indictment to be refreshed by the overwhelming thought—the reality—that God had forgiven us even before we asked. That justice was not his *métier*, but mercy his abundant gift.

She looked at me, clear-eyed, her hands folded so reverently before her, the first-Communion posture those same nuns, at once caring and yet so misguided, had taught.

I placed a shard of holy, broken bread on her tongue. Her head slowly dropped to her chest, her chin touching just where the porta-cath bulged from beneath her protruding collarbone, etched against skin so pale. I stood there, my head bowed, longer than I usually do. When I raised my head, there was Jane, standing unsteadily before me, her arm against the wall for support. Tears cascaded over her cheeks. She reached out to embrace me, her arms trembling. "You've made me very happy today," she said, pressing her cheeks to mine, sharing these tears of gratitude, of God's release from the hidden illness that had plagued her for more than half a century.

I held her thin frame tightly to me for a moment, and then eased her back into the chair. Her face, so pensive and blank when I had come in just minutes before, was glowing.

Closer to Home

It's usually not difficult for me to tell why most patients are in the hospital. If wires spiral out of their loose-fitting hospital gown, something is amiss with their heart. An IV pole with small, clear bags means they are being treated for cancer. If they are lying pillowless and flat: back or neck surgery. A cast on an arm or leg protects bones reset after an accident or surgically altered in the operating room.

As best I can, I try to identify with each person, to put myself in his or her place. To feel the fear that accompanies the feeling of pressure in a shoulder or tingling in an arm that signals a heart attack, the awful nausea of cancer-killing drugs, the phantom pain of a newly amputated leg. Perhaps it's only a feeble attempt at method-acting ministry, but I want to be as close as I can to their experience to better serve them.

Midway through my visits on a steamy Thursday morning in July, I didn't have to conjure up any such sympathetic feelings with the fortyish woman in Room 641. Just by the way she lay there, I felt I knew. When I instinctively took her hand as we began to talk—and she began to explain why she wasn't worthy to receive Communion—I became sure.

Her hand was limp. When she moved her head to look at me, it was locked in slow-motion mode. Her dazed eyes seemed at once to see me and to look right through me. Her body sank into the mattress as if melted by some evil, extraterrestrial force. I knew all the signs. They added up to the same diagnosis a young navy neurologist had pronounced over me as I lay, similarly limp, in a hospital many years before.

One morning, aboard my ship, as I shaved in the tiny mirror in my equally tiny junior officer's stateroom, my vision suddenly blurred. I peered into the mirror to watch as one eye moved smartly to the right and the other lazily followed, finally catching up and bringing clear vision once more. My left side had been feeling numb and tingly for weeks, but I was otherwise healthy, twenty-five-years old, and paid no attention to it. Yes, that symptom would pass, the newly board-certified neurologist said when I asked him. But then? He went no further, but the answer was already on his face. It would return. By then I had read the literature. The attacks would become more and more severe. I would begin to drop things and stumble. The disease would unpredictably and coyly leave me alone, only to return. And become more and more severe. I would be turned into a rag doll, my muscles useless.

This was multiple sclerosis, and there was no cure.

Elaine also must have started out with a distant early warning, something as seemingly innocuous and passing, but MS took further hold in her body (whereas it went no further in mine) and continued its vengeful, unforgiving path. "Oh, I haven't been to church. I just can't take Communion," Elaine said, the recalcitrant muscles in her face mustering a small smile.

Had God been keeping count of her church attendance? The Great Computer in the Sky taking in the data and rendering a negative verdict? "Elaine, what kind of God wouldn't come to you when you need God most?" I asked, quietly. She lay there, silent.

"The Eucharist isn't a reward for good behavior," I said, holding her hand a bit more tightly. "It's food for the journey of life. Your food." I looked at her. She slowly closed her eyes, lost in thought.

I never would really know the sickness in her body, but I knew well the sickness in her soul—that aching soul sickness that cauterizes hope and snuffs the eternal flame within us. The leaden sensation that makes each day a burden to be borne. In my own life, I knew its painful pall all too well. When God seemed beyond reach, when death seemed the only and merciful answer to a meaningless life.

I had said the words so many times at Mass: "Lord, I am not worthy to receive you, but only say the word, and my soul shall be healed." What does that mean exactly? And what was that word? I have thought about that for many years. I think the "word" God pronounces is "now." Don't wait another second. Come to me so that I might embrace you. My love for you transcends anything you have done or will do. I cannot do anything but love you, because I created you; you are my own. Come to me. Come where nothing can harm you. Come where no disease can touch you. Come where you are whole again because you are united in me, and I in you. Now.

Perhaps it's because I was spared the ravages of this horrible disease, only to go on to live too many years away from God and myself, that I wanted Elaine to know that not only was she not outside God's love and worthy to take the holy Eucharist, but that she was, in fact, the most worthy, the most loved. Is it such a stretch of the imagination to plumb the mind of a God who would send "his only son" to earth to show us a way to live, only to have that son crucified by the rule-makers and the righteous? Would God not offer comfort immediately to those crucified each day, each hour by their own demons, their own sense of worthlessness, by a horrible affliction like multiple sclerosis?

"Elaine, he's here. Now. Waiting for you. Wanting to be with you," I found myself saying. "Hoping that you won't mistake rules for love. What kind of God would see his daughter lying here and just pass her by? We're Catholics, and we are the worst at knowing the Bible," I hesitated, and she smiled with me, "but that story about the Good Samaritan. He couldn't—just couldn't—pass by a person in need. Would God do any less for any of us?"

The few Scripture passages I knew well tumbled into my mind. I had read them aloud in previous visits and now could recite them almost by heart. The woman Christ met at the well and promised a new kind of water from which she would never again be thirsty. The confused apostles on the road to Emmaus who could not recognize the man walking beside them as Christ and would only later recall, "Were not our hearts burning within us while he spoke to us on the way?" And when Christ blessed and broke bread with them, all fear, all doubt, was gone. They knew.

I held the pyx in my closed hand. Within was the bread of life. Within was the power of God.

"Lord, we are heartily sorry for those things in our lives we have done that have not pleased you—or us—and for things we have left undone," I went on, following the classic act of contrition form but shaping words and thoughts as best I could to fit the moment. "And Elaine and I know that even before we name our sins, they are forgiven. Bless this good woman and prepare her to receive you in the most intimate and wonderful way. Not tomorrow. Not after she does this or says that. Now."

I removed the host from the pyx and held it before her. The dull light from the window, filtered by the Venetian blinds half-closed, bathed her face in a rich glow. "This is the Lamb of God who takes away the sins of the world, happy are those of us called to this, his eternal banquet. O Lord, I am not worthy to receive you, but say the word...only say the word...and I know that you will, and I will, be healed, Elaine. Healed."

I placed the host on her tongue. She closed her eyes. I stood there a few moments. I touched her shoulder before leaving the room, quietly closing the door behind me.

Lessons in Smallness

If I've left the impression that I enter each hospital room on the wings of holy Love, God's appointed messenger with heart unblemished and glowing, all human concerns, judgments, and prejudices cast aside, I must make a confession.

It's not true.

There are patients I immediately like and others I dislike. There are those whose names on my list make me want to turn around and go home, calling in sick myself—or, at a minimum, to conveniently miss them on my rounds. The venal, selfish, hypercritical man who lives the other one-hundred sixty hours each week outside these hospital hallways is the same man who walks them each week.

It does not escape me, as I reflect on well over a decade of hospital visits, that while I have gained insights and graces, I probably am no less purified because of my hospital experiences. I know this because, even with all the remorse I hold for past offenses and mumbling an unbroken string of firm purposes of amendment, when I come across someone who I think has wronged me (or ranks anywhere on a continuum of the unduly unkind to the downright mean), it is no less a struggle.

And I can be even smaller than that. There is a Catholic nurse I know whose frantic movements on the floor annoy me. She is always in a hurry. Always has the same, inane comments about my children or hers, never seems to have a moment to pause and talk about anything meaningful. I see her down the hallway and detour to the other side. I perfunctorily nod and offer nothing when we do pass. I have tried in the past to offer a short half-sentence, only to have her dash away. The pouch at my waist contains the loving gift of the Eucharist; its bearer is an icy, hateful numbskull.

Then there will be patients, members of my own parish, who I know dislike me. I am a voluble man, all too willing to offer thoughts on just about anything, not always conventional in my life or Catholic practice. For those who hew closer to the accepted path, I am fingernails on a blackboard, windblown sand in the eye, irritating static on a classical-music radio station.

So there he was on a Thursday morning, offering an opportunity to transcend my worst self. He and his wife were pillars of the parish, daily communicants, and also some of the meaner people around. He never missed a chance to take a snipe at me, whether it was about something I'd written, one of my commentaries on the local NPR station, or the mere fact that I was walking into church on Sunday morning, apostate (in his eyes) that I was.

After a minor surgical procedure he was feeling pretty well and was about to go home, so he was his usual pithy self, making some

kind of snide remark about the quality of eucharistic ministers—
namely, low. Namely, me.

I smiled weakly and said the accepted prayers. In other circumstances, I might have proclaimed God's love for "this good man" or
talked of the "beautiful gift of his presence with us today," but my
heart was too hardened. I departed with a weak smile. I went to the
stairwell and paused.

A year before, someone, I think from my parish, had called the
diocesan offices after an announcement came out in our monthly
Catholic magazine that I would be the speaker for an upcoming
stewardship conference. I had spoken on the subject throughout the
country and had created a stewardship kit for churches to use. This
anonymous call led to my speaking engagement being canceled. The
reason: something I had once written in one of my books.

Whoever had reported me had pulled a few sentences out of context to indict me. The bishop in a neighboring diocese got wind of it
and said he would forbid anyone in his jurisdiction from attending.
Speaking engagement canceled.

Was this man I had just visited the one who had reported me?
Or was it one of the others I have visited and given Communion to
who I know bitterly disagrees with me? Of course I will never know.
But this is precisely the kind of moment with which I am—we all
are—presented day after day. We are allowed to make a choice: to
forgive real or imagined slights and hurts or to remain hardened to
the wellspring of God's love that lies just below the surface of this
encounter, to break out of our half-baked notion of God's love.

I realized I had once again chosen the road most traveled, the
easy road, the road of retribution. I'd given him the Eucharist, but

I'd held back myself. I did what was required, nothing more. What a hollow, sour feeling it left within me.

I would like to say that I changed after that day, but there were subsequent visits that proved I had not. As I prayed each week in the hospital chapel before my rounds, I might have asked God to walk with me. But too often I left God in the hallway when I went into a room of someone I sourly kept choosing to dislike.

Some months afterwards, I entered Room 723 and found an unfamiliar name on my list. When I saw who it was, I stopped short. She was huddled in an almost fetal position, the look on her normally pinched face even more pronounced than I remembered it. She looked up at me and said nothing. I took it for a glare. As I came closer, I could see that it was pain contorting her thin, lined face.

Sue had a minor supervisory job at the university where I was teaching, but a position that required virtually everyone to pass through her jurisdiction. And she made it hard on everyone. There were no simple matters that could be dealt with quickly. Not with Sue. There was always a problem with the paperwork, the packaging, the timing. Her small staff was always too busy. She was always too busy. We patrons were a burden. She had made my life a living hell as I tried to administer a grant.

I doubt that she recognized me. I was but a tiny, passing annoyance, but I certainly recognized and remembered her.

She began to speak. Her voice was hoarse, familiar, irritating. All I could think about was her gruff treatment, her meanness and obstinacy. I was not listening to her words, just playing out the old script I knew so well and hung on to so tenaciously. And after all, why shouldn't I dislike her? She was an awful person.

A few words hovering in the still, stale air began poking at my protective layer of self-righteous disdain. Forty years of smoking. Lung cancer. Horrible pain. Gasping for every breath. I successfully deflected them. So many more patients to see. Let's get this over with.

I took out the pyx and was ready to say the required prayer and be on my way. There was a lone host at the bottom. I reached for it. My hand paused. Sue was talking in that raspy voice, each agony of her life encapsulated in a short burst of words before she inhaled deeply, gulping in another breath. There before me in the pyx was Jesus Christ, silent, alone, in the form of the humblest piece of bread at my fingertips. Jesus Christ, God and mortal being, who struggled with his own humanity, even as he felt the divine within him. Jesus Christ, who gave and gave and gave still more. Bitter with his sleeping followers, crushed that one of them would betray him, he nonetheless offered himself on the cross for the wretched as well as the good.

I looked up from the pyx. And the words slowly began to penetrate.

She was such a lonely woman. It was so apparent as she talked about how she tried her best to cope with her illness after her retirement from the university. Her life had been that job, her link to the world outside a small, rented apartment. Unmarried, with no apparent family, her life had obviously not been a happy one. Her bitterness was deeply rooted in still other hurts and disappointments I would never know and could only imagine.

But then she spoke with such pride of her work, how her staff performed their services so well, how she tried so hard to serve her customers, even with budget cuts and difficult employees, poor equipment and inadequate space. And the air-conditioning unit. It never

75

worked right, freezing in winter, malfunctioning in hot weather. But her job was her calling, and she was devoted to it. She had given her all. There was little left over. Her proudest possession was a pin acknowledging her decades of service.

I looked down at the single host once more. She exhaled audibly. With her, I took the next, deep breath.

"Lord Jesus Christ, here is Sue," I began my prayer. "She served many, many people over her years at the university. You were always there for her. Now, Lord, hold this good woman in your most tender embrace this day. Pass your comforting hands over her lungs so that they take in this good, sweet air. And let Sue feel the peace that only you can give, the healing only you can provide, the rest for our weary souls, the love that does pass all understanding. Let this be a good, restful day for Sue. Let her feel your warm, loving presence in this precious gift, the Eucharist. And let her know that you never leave this bedside, and any time day or night she can look up, and you will be here, smiling upon her. For she is your precious daughter, and you love her so much. This is the Lamb of God who..."

Her face, contorted in pain, softened. She closed her eyes to receive the host.

I walked down the hallway and paused once again in the stairwell. I looked out to the new day coming into being, the sun dappling the drab, gray walls of the parking garage, the line of bare trees beyond. I prayed. This time I prayed for myself. That I might unlock, unblock my own heart. That I, who had just spoken those words in Room 723, might hear them myself. That I might be open to God's forgiving, healing power. That I might do better in the days ahead.

Redemption

There are days when I should pause more thoughtfully before entering the hospital's revolving door. If I insist on continuing, I should look still deeper into my own heart. Realizing what I have found, I should reverse my course and head back to the parking lot.

For I am in no state of mind or soul to be of much help to anyone—tired, overloaded with things that have to be done that day, worried about one or both of my sons, concerned about my precarious finances, angry at somebody—the multiple-choice list is long, covering a wide range of daily agonies. God's courier? The bearer of God's presence and grace? My heart is hard; the fruits of my spiritual garden desiccated. After all, this is a volunteer assignment I have taken on. Can't I just unvolunteer myself today?

I enter the lobby, scan the list of patients to see, and make a silent, unspoken pledge: I'll get through this as quickly as possible. God smiles at my plan. God's not about to allow that to happen. God has some surprises in store.

It was on such a day that I started my rounds on the ninth floor. My latest fantastic, prescient, seminal idea for a book had just been summarily rejected. My bank account was teetering on the thin edge between black and red. Tracy had to have a root canal. Daniel's and Noah's tuition payments were due. Workers who had come to assess damage on my garage roof found not only rotted wood but also a handsome colony of termites. My back was aching, memories of that L4-L5 laminectomy twenty years before. Oy vey. Woe is me.

And who was my first patient—a good, worthy soul? Terry was in his forties or fifties (it was hard to tell because he was so ravaged by drug use), in the hospital for a severe infection from intravenous injections of heroin, cocaine, or if I could believe him as he rattled on, just about any mood-altering substance he could get his hands on and then mainline. He was too old to still be using drugs; he was too much of a wise guy to get much sympathy from me.

He thought he was being humorous when he made fun of the starched headpieces the sisters in his grade school wore. "Squeezed their brains, those goofy broads," was his analysis. And the priests who drank too much and seemed to have better cars than anybody else in the parish. "Tell me they weren't dipping in the till for that." And, moving on to the parishioners, "We were like dumb cattle; they told us what to do and we did it; what crap!"

Did he want the Eucharist? "Sure, why not?" as if I were standing in a supermarket aisle offering him a free sample of organic apple juice or turkey burger.

"Oh, Lord, look down on this good man Terry, and bring him the comfort of this great gift of your own loving and powerful self that he might be healed and from this moment on, set out on a better path in life, with you at his side." That was the prayer I should have said.

Instead, I yanked a host from the pyx, "ThisistheLambofGodwhotakesawaythesinsoftheworld" (quick breath) "happyarethosewhoarecalledtothishiseternalbanquet." I placed the host on Terry's tongue.

I looked down, already impatiently eyeing the next name on the list. The room was quiet. I was ready for some other smart remark. Nothing. I looked up. Terry's eyes were flooded with tears.

"Oh, my God—" Sobs choked off any more words. The tears streamed down over his pronounced cheekbones, negotiating the stubble of beard before falling gently on his reverently folded hands.

I put my own hands, hardly as reverent, over his.

"He is with you. And he's going to stay with you," I said.

"I know that," he said, when he could again speak. "He's always been there. Thanks," he said, now tentatively putting his quaking hands over mine. "You don't know what this means to me."

I held onto him for at least a minute, neither of us speaking. I quietly left the room.

Oh, my God. The cry of the ages: simple, unvarnished, unashamed, direct.

I was supposed to be Terry's salvation. But who needed saving here? I was to offer him redemption, only I was the one who was redeemed. I was appointed to inform him of the power of faith, but he taught me what true faith really was about. That morning, Terry breathed a soul into this impatient robot of a man.

That is the mystery of God, of the Eucharist, of God's presence in the world. God showers graces with such reckless abandon and quixotic unpredictability. God takes those of us, the smugly religious who think we know God and are close to God, and introduces us to the truly religious, the beloved, the lost sheep Jesus came to save and savor.

My own hardened heart would be touched by God's gentle ways many more times in the days ahead.

Ed was an ex-New Jersey policeman: Irish, tough, and obviously away from the Church for many years. No Eucharist for him. He ran down the litany of Catholicism's excesses—condemning a soul to hell for a Friday hamburger, the brutality of the confessional at the hands of an insensitive priest, and lately, the sexual abuse of minors.

"Give me something to disagree with you about," I replied, smiling. These were hardly impediments to receiving the Eucharist, I told him. He wasn't alone. But that wasn't the total accounting of the Catholic Church. There was more, much more. "Here is Christ; let's not let all that business keep you from him. He breaks through everything. This is a *divine* gift; those are *human* failings."

No, he didn't want to receive, he said gruffly. He was a man used to giving and taking orders and making himself clear. I had a busy day and a long list of patients. I wasn't in the mood to try to crack open this hard shell. Might I say a prayer? He assented with a nod. Where the words would come from, I didn't know.

I took out a host and held it before him. I stared at the tiny cross impressed at the center. It always helped focus me, remembering just what this host contained. "Lord, here is Ed. He was a fair cop; you can just see it in his face. He helped people even when they might not have deserved it. He went through some tough times on the job. He tried to be fair. It wasn't always easy, but he gave it his best. Tough guy, sure. Never a bully. A big difference; we both know that.

"Well, Lord, right now, he needs you to take care of him. To let those tests come back with good results. That the cancer is at bay. That he can rest assured you are with him whatever happens. You are like the buddy on the beat, when your partner is in trouble, you are right there. The backup. You are here, right now, in this tiny piece of bread, as real as you were two thousand years ago to your friends when they needed you. Now bless Ed, Lord, and make this a good, restful, and healing day for him. Amen."

I was about to return the host to the pyx.

"I'll take that," he blurted out. I looked up. The tough guy's face had softened, those piercing blue eyes held me as sure as handcuffs. "This is the Lamb of God," I recited. I placed the host on his tongue. His eyes closed. I paused for a moment, then silently left the room.

I'll take that. Must not God be overjoyed with this leap of faith and trust? Did that host glow before Ed's blue eyes? Was there a soft murmuring he alone heard? Who knows? But does not God beckon us in so many ways to come just as we are? And there, in Room 709, with God so close to Ed in the Eucharist, was there not a connection made? Perhaps in heaven we will be able to see the now-invisible rivers of grace flowing all around us. Ed chose to drink from that holy river. And he made me, who had been ready to move on, pause and allow the wonder of God to be experienced.

Some patients are voluble and open, like Ed and Terry, each in their own way to be sure. Others are harder to communicate with. Their pain, their natural shyness—whatever is on their minds drives them still deeper into themselves when they are in a hospital bed.

So it was with Janet in Room 609. My attempts at the simplest conversation were rebuffed. I kept hitting a wall, and so I decided to dispatch with Janet and to move on to more promising terrain. Yes, she wanted to receive.

I said, "Lord, here is Janet. She approaches your altar with outstretched hands, seeking your healing power, your love, the mighty wings under which we can be secure and find shelter."

I placed the host on her tongue. I had spent perhaps three minutes in the room. I began to leave. Her voice was so low I could barely hear her.

"That's the nicest thing a priest has ever done for me," she said. "Thank you for coming to visit me."

"I'm not a priest, Janet. I'm a eucharistic minister. You're a member of the family. We wouldn't have missed you for anything. It was my pleasure, Janet, an honor." I found myself stumbling over my words. "He's with you now. You can be sure of that."

The nicest thing. Ever. A three-minute visit with a shy woman whose missing teeth and near-empty room spoke of a hard life where nothing came easy or free. Except this beautiful gift.

God's nature revealed. Once more. Redemption for both of us.

Uncharted
Pathways

Adán, the Million-Dollar Man

It is rare that I have a long-term relationship with my patients. Most are in for a day or two and then mercifully out of the hospital. Adán was different. I was with him for a long time, and while we couldn't understand each other's earthly words, we somehow seemed to communicate in a more universal language.

Adán was one of the millions of undocumented immigrants who come north to the United States seeking work and a better life. He was a cheery fellow, a full, round face, curly, unkempt hair, and a more-than-ample belly: a Mexican Buddha. He was also an alcoholic, and each time one of his array of chronic medical problems was under control or resolved—pneumonia, erratic heartbeat, diabetes, mononucleosis, tuberculosis, and a gastric ulcer, to name just a few—he would be released from the hospital to go out and abuse his body still more.

I visited him in a regular hospital room, in isolation, and in intensive care. I nicknamed him the Million-Dollar Man because his medical bills added up to at least that. It is a tribute to the American medical system that he was cared for so well, even though he might not have been considered worthy, undocumented drunkard that he was. But when I mumbled my few words of limited Spanish— "*Amigo! Buenos dias. ¿Cómo está usted? ¿Qué pasa? De la iglesia*" was my quite limited range—his smile was, to use the wrong word in this context, contagious.

Each time he was readmitted, his overall situation worsened, and gradually his once-healthy bronze skin grew sallow and his bright eyes seemed to recede further into his skull. I stood with the Spanish-speaking social worker, trying to convince Adán to mend his ways, but we both knew his "*Sí, sí, sí*" was only to please us, hardly with—as we Catholics know the phrase so well—a "firm purpose of amendment." The few friends who occasionally stopped by during his early hospital stays fell away. Adán was becoming more of a burden than they, with their own tenuous grip on survival, wanted to bear. By the time he was in intensive care, on life support, he was alone.

Intensive care units are medical miracles of technology and biological micromanagement, visited by physicians who adroitly address the organ or condition that falls under their specialty, but staffed hour-by-hour by nurses who care for the whole person. Their dedication and focus earn them an alarming burnout rate, the highest among hospital medical professionals. Adán was admitted with a bleeding ulcer—the result of his latest binge—compounded by so many other ailments that this time the dominos tumbled quickly. One day he was sitting up in bed, eating his breakfast, and the next day he was comatose.

His face was so swollen and bloated when I opened the glass door to Cubicle 5 in the medical intensive care unit that if I hadn't known what he looked like before, I wouldn't have recognized him. An endotracheal breathing tube was taped to his cheek. The green flickering line on a telemetry monitor showed the broad, slow, lazy waveform of a dying man rather than the normal sharp waves of the living. A mechanical ventilator sustained his breathing, its regular rhythm a false promise.

After a series of strokes, his vital organs no longer were receiving the blood flow they needed to survive. His body was shutting down; the toxins were no longer being removed. His flesh was breaking down, in effect rotting. His temperature continued to rise. The brain scan showed no more than occasional, primal activity. He was clearly dying.

Adán had reached the point where there would be no more medical triumphs. Nothing more could be done. As for end-of-life instructions, there were none. A series of cross hatches through his name on the census board on the wall indicated he was not to be resuscitated if his heart stopped beating. But the mechanical ventilator steadily pumped on. This could go on for days. The MICU staff knew what the next step should be, but who would agree to it?

There was Jaime, a brother or cousin or not even kin—I never could sort this out. Adán's family in Mexico had long ago written him off. Adán had made it known that, when he died, he wanted to be buried in the Mexican village of his birth.

I stood beside his bed, two intensive care nurses with me, and looked at his mortal self heaving fitfully. His eyes bulged. To call them bloodshot would be inaccurate; they were flooded with blood. Internally, the bleeding was so massive that blood leaked out of his mouth, soaking layers of gauze, a collar of crimson around the breathing tube. We would wait another day.

I remembered the first time I had seen him, when he was just a normal, healthy-looking alcoholic with a liver worn out from the pace of his dusk-to-dawn, dawn-to-dusk drinking. Getting the point across that I was from the Church, I showed him the host. He received that first time tentatively, I thought. His eyes were open, flickering nervously as if he were unsure what was happening or what he should do about it. It may have only been his second Communion, the first being so many years ago, a rite of passage in Mexican Catholic life that was not necessarily repeated. So many Mexicans I visited had not been churchgoers, although they would bridle at being called anything other than Catholic. They were Catholic to the core, if not by the book.

While we couldn't really communicate in a mutual language, our facial expressions—and the Eucharist—seemed to fill in the gaps. I would come into his room each time with a look of mock surprise on my face, as if I had just come around a corner and run into an old friend. He would hide his face in his hands, grinning all the time, feigning his shame at being in the hospital still another time.

His reception of the Eucharist grew in intensity, need, and indeed beauty as he grew sicker. The tentativeness went quickly, and he would look longingly at the black pouch as we talked, as if it held the answer to all his life's problems. He made the Sign of the Cross, and his hand would then go to his lips, the *amen* of the Latino world.

First, his eyes would close, trusting that what would be placed on his tongue was for his benefit and that there was nothing expected of him. Then he would mumble a few words that I couldn't understand, his private communiqué to El Señor. He would be lost in thought as I quietly left the room.

The last time I gave him the Eucharist he seemed at peace, the ingratiating smile of a supplicant had turned into the calm face of an accepted son at table with his father. Actually, we said less and less each time. There was no need to attempt such foolish banter; the stakes were too high, the time too short.

The funeral director called me the next day. Adán had died. The funeral director had tried to reach the next of kin on Adán's record, but the number was disconnected. The address was outside the city, in a poor area where migrant workers lived. The funeral director had called the hospital, and they had referred him to me. Yes, someone had signed the release to allow the removal of life support, but they couldn't reach him either. What should be done with the body? He could simply cremate it, but what do with the remains?

Adán had lived such a marginal life; I just couldn't let him go like this. What would it cost to have a memorial service? The price started at about three thousand dollars, but eventually was whittled down to a thousand. The basics: closed cardboard coffin, no viewing. I had some money left over from a previous project and pitched in most of the cost, allowing Jaime, who eventually resurfaced, to take up a collection for the rest. My pastor, Father John Gillespie, agreed to hold the memorial service in one of the anterooms at the funeral home.

Jaime was supposed to bring some clothes for the viewing, but they never appeared. The funeral director was on the phone hourly as the time for the service neared. I called Sister Isaac, the wonderful nun who heads our parish social ministry outreach, gave her the rough size, and an hour later I appeared at the funeral home with a gray pinstripe suit (its lapels a few seasons out of fashion), white shirt, and a fine, silk tie. The funeral director looked quizzically at me, then disappeared.

Later in the afternoon Jaime appeared, having rounded up a few of his buddies. There was no mention of sending Adán back to Mexico. "I know this is what he wanted," Jaime assured me. Father Gillespie, who had never laid eyes on Adán before this moment, was wise enough to turn over the eulogy to the half-dozen mourners. They were dressed in their best shirts—one with a half-naked woman splayed across the back—cowboy boots, and the faint smell of cheap whiskey. And there was Adán, looking like a stockbroker in his gray pinstripes, his face still puffy, his neck exceeding the collar size by an inch or two, but artfully finessed by the funeral director. This same funeral director also provided a wooden coffin for the viewing; the cardboard would hold him for the cremation, but it "looked so cheap, I couldn't do it," he whispered to me.

In broken English, his friends talked most about their great times with Adán, whose life in this summary seemed a string of great payday meals and boozy weekend nights. But Adán was always the first one up in the morning, hungover or not, waking the others so they would get to work on time. I mentioned our many visits, the holy Eucharist that Adán received with such reverence, how he blessed himself and then pressed his knuckles to his lips for the amen. Father Gillespie was inspired to say that Adán obviously had a heart for God and was now with him in heaven, relieved of the passing burdens of this world to enjoy the eternal happiness of the next. We said the Our Father together and filed out.

I was alone with the funeral director as he closed the coffin and wheeled it toward the door, where the transfer to the cardboard coffin would take place. The cremation would follow.

"Want the suit back?" he asked.

"He looked pretty good in it, don't you think?"

"Up to you; just going to. ..."

"I know, I know. I think we should let him go out in style."

Married/Not-Quite Married

When I walk into a room at the hospital and see what I assume to be a husband or wife at a spouse's bedside—and ascertain in the course of my visit that they are indeed married—I ask if they are Catholic. When the answer is no, I might feign shock and act as though I'm leaving the room. "Not Catholic!" There are many such couples of different faiths, and they immediately get the little joke. I'll quickly follow up with, "I think we're worshiping the same God. At least, the last time I looked."

I might say these words with a certain lightness, but I believe them quite seriously. "When we get to heaven, I don't think he'll be calling us Methodist or Baptist or Catholic. My beloved son, my cherished daughter, is what we're going to hear," I often say during my prayer. I was raised in a Catholic Church that believed it alone had the key to the kingdom. Then, thankfully, the Second Vatican Council took that master key to the ecumenical hardware store and made enough copies for all sincere believers in the One, True God.

As I was growing into adulthood in the 1950s and early 1960s, we were living in an idyllic *Leave It to Beaver* era when Mom and Dad—white and vaguely Protestant, of course—and their two and a half children were the American standard. We who didn't fit the mold felt something was missing. Of course, family life was never like that. Relationships were always more conflicted and complicated. Then came the ensuing decades where, some contend, our societal grid was shattered. Other voices maintain that finally the lines on the field were widened to allow more players to participate openly, legally. Whatever side you happen to be on, we all witnessed the once-sacrosanct definition of *family* being rewritten.

On one occasion I drew back in mock horror at the Methodist man married to a Catholic woman who was recovering from a severe aneurysm. The husband's knowing smile at first puzzled me. However, when I began my prayers and he made a perfect Sign of the Cross, followed the Hail Mary word for word, and mouthed "this is the Lamb of God..." I slowly began to see the beauty of this dual-religion, fifty-one–year marriage. He was a Methodist in name and weekly service attendance; he was a better Catholic than most of us.

He had agreed to raise the children Catholic and had done so with a positive spirit. He had enriched himself, drinking at both these fountains of faith.

For Catholic couples of fifty, sixty, or even seventy years of married life, Eucharist received in a bare hospital room, as the days remaining for one of them are likely few, is especially poignant. I can picture many older couples, hand in hand, as I said the prayers and offered the hosts, so beautifully and blessedly brought together once again in their hour of need with the Friend who witnessed their wedding day and every day since.

In Room 823, on a bone-chilling winter's day, the dignified man with a full hair of meticulously combed, brilliant white hair looked down so lovingly at his wife. She struggled to swallow even the tiny shard of host I had given her. Her cheekbones held taut skin like a tent pole supporting a piece of thin, opaque canvas. Her eyes, a murky blue, were sunken in her face. The bare outlines of her body barely gave rise to the sheets.

"Isn't she beautiful," he said as we looked down at her.

He didn't see a body wasted by lymphoma, a hip broken in a cruel fall. He saw the lovely slip of a girl who came down the aisle with such dignity on her father's arm in a cavernous Bronx church so many years before. He saw her soul, brilliant and whole, for nothing could harm that in any way. He saw her with the eyes of love. He saw her with God's own eyes, as God sees the real us.

Some marriages, though long in duration, have seen pain and discord beyond the normal spats and difficulties all unions must weather. That was so obvious as I stood beside the bed of Bernice, her husband Anthony off to the side, his arms limp. The pictures on the nightstand showed a beautiful Italian woman with luxuriant auburn hair. The woman in the bed bore some facial resemblance, but her hair was pitifully patchy and thin, a faint whisper. I asked Anthony to draw near the bed as we prayed together, but when I offered him the Eucharist, he said no.

"I haven't been the best guy," he said. He filled in some of the details as we talked in the hallway outside her room. He played the trombone and had to travel to earn a living. Late nights, too many drinks, and adoring women—Anthony was ashamed to admit it wasn't only once or twice.

On that and subsequent visits, as Bernice grew thinner and sicker, I tried to convince Anthony that the past was past, and God had a terribly short memory for our failings. Each week I affirmed Anthony's obvious love for his wife, and God's love for him, a love that blots out and forgives anything that we might have done. Nevertheless, Anthony resisted until one morning, when his wife was about to be released, to go home to die, that she looked up at him, so tenderly, and said these simple words: "You are the best guy, Anthony. You're my best guy."

He cried. I cried. Bernice cried. I took out the pyx. Why not, my look told Anthony. Why not?

Anthony, with closed eyes, received the Eucharist after all those years wandering, hungering in the desert, after having done whatever he had done but feeling the weight of his guilt far beyond anything Our Lord ever would want him to bear. His wife's words had healed him. Christ's presence could now warm him and prepare him for the days ahead in which he would witness her further decline. The Eucharist had brought them together, released his tears, inspired his wife's loving words. Anthony would later tell me he had gone to his parish priest to confess whatever sins had plagued him. Would all this have happened if not for the powerful, pervasive, embracing grace of God contained in that humble wafer?

Then there are the "not-quite married" couples I visit. There are many reasons that this is their state in life. It could be that one of them couldn't obtain an annulment, and the only real marriage they know is in the Catholic Church. Even with all the pain this procedure might cause them, if they couldn't have a Catholic wedding, there would be no wedding at all. Or there are just too many children, and too many countervailing forces, to blend all the pieces neatly together. Social security payments, a house that won't sell, relatives who are scandalized by a previous divorce or divorces.

They themselves are often racked with guilt that they are not legally and religiously married. They cannot cavalierly brush aside everything they learned in their Catholic upbringing. I try as best I can to pray with them, holding up what is usually so apparent and palpable. Such was what I found as I stood in a ninth floor room with Bill and Marge.

They had been together for over fifteen years, but not at peace. They acknowledged that they always felt outside the Church, that they were sinners. Their background was complicated: aging parents, a mentally ill child, angry ex-spouses. "It was the best we could do. We tried, but we didn't quite do it right."

"Very few of us do," I replied. "Let's pray together."

"Yours is a beautiful love for one another and it shows today," I began my prayer, looking first at Marge, then at Bill. "You have made your relationship holy; you have sanctified it with your love. That is demonstrated here, today. So tender. So real. So beautiful. Here is your good man, Marge, right beside you. Would he, could he be anywhere else? No. And on this side, Christ. You are joined in a way that in his infinite wisdom he understands. Maybe other people don't understand; you may not even understand. But he understands completely and he wants to be with you this morning, to shower his blessings on you. Now, here, take and eat, this is his Body, offered for us. Be strengthened, knowing how desperately he cares for you. Happy are those who are called to this, his eternal banquet."

On one morning, my journeys among the "almost married" brought me into Bob's room, 632. Standing beside his bed was not a Ruth or a Becky or a Sue—but a Bill. What was I to do? These two men—the expression of their love "intrinsically disordered" as my Church pronounced in the Congregation for the Doctrine of the Faith's *Persona Humana* (section VIII)—were obviously living together. What I could do, and did do, before anything else, was listen to their story.

Bill looked like a robust, burly truck driver. Bob, measured and slight of frame, had been a bank executive. They were obviously devoted to each other. Bill had rented a yacht because Bob wanted to go fishing during one of the brief periods of remission from his advancing cancer. Bill took Bob to Catholic Mass each Sunday, with wheelchair or crutches, even physically cradling him in his arms and carrying him to a back pew. He bathed him, changed his soiled bed, and cooked whatever Bob even mentioned he might like to eat.

I slowly took the pyx from my pouch and withdrew two hosts. They bowed their heads.

"This is the Lamb of God, who takes away the sins of the world. The Lamb of God who offered himself for you two, as you offer yourself to each other in love. God knows the depth of that love and what you mean to each other. God is the God of love, and that love is with you both today, in a special and real way. In this." I held the two hosts in the air. The Body of Christ. I then gave one host to Bill and one to Bob.

Later that morning as I was walking out of the hospital, I found myself reflecting on the patients I had seen. Had I been too casual with distributing the Eucharist? Had I overlooked things I should have noticed? Should I have been more careful?

There on a bench was Bob, smoking a cigarette. Irony of ironies, as his beloved Bill was dying of lung cancer. We started talking, and he told me of his marriage and his three children he and Bob saw often. Of he and Bob meeting on the job so many years before and falling in love, a love neither of them wanted, a love that at first repelled them both. But a love so strong it could not be denied, a love that had lasted over twenty-five years.

I looked at Bob, his droopy mustache flecked with gray, his bloodhound's eyes so sad. I reached out, took his hand and held it, saying nothing. No, it was not casual at all to give them the Eucharist. There is nothing casual about human love, about God's love. God had blessed them. And God wanted them to know it that day.

Touching and Knowing

Maude was only in her late forties, I estimated, but she had already battled the disease for three years. She was propped up in bed, two pillows behind her, more poisons in the clear bag on the IV pole draining into her body. Her face was flushed and unsmiling.

She was so brave. She was so sick, so alone. She told me of her long struggle with cancer, her rage at the diagnosis ("God, what is this: I'm a good person. Why are you doing this to me?"), the friends and relatives who stood by her, those who could not bear her agony and turned away. She had finally found that the rage only gnawed at her resolve and undermined her relationship with God. That relationship was far too important, and it not only mended, but deepened and became stronger than ever before. She was at peace. The cancer would triumph. She would die.

Looking down at Maude, I thought back to the strict schooling I received in my training session. I was to carefully find out if the person was in the state of grace, a "practicing" Catholic. I was to say the assigned prayers without deviation. I was to retrieve the Eucharist from my church and proceed immediately to the hospital without a stop. I was to—I was to—I was to.

I did as I was told for the first few visits fourteen years ago, but I soon found I was not good at walking this ritualistic tightrope. I began to improvise in my prayers. I refused to be the Grand Inquisitor as to the state of their souls or level of Catholic praxis. Moreover, I found that simply standing by the side of the bed, without touching my patients, simply was against my nature. Who would not want to hug or touch these courageous women and men?

Maude had a rosary on her table, and I added another, a simple plastic rosary made by poor women in Kochi, India, near an orphanage I accidentally came across years ago and to which I regularly return to volunteer. I told Maude of the place and these women and that the prayers they whispered while stringing this rosary would now be sent heavenward each time she fingered the beads. I prayed that she would have a restful, pain-free day, a good appetite—even with the chemotherapy—and that she would be able to go home to her loved ones just as soon as possible.

I gave her the host and stood there, as I always do, in silence. I looked up into her sad, pain-filled eyes. I leaned across the bed and softly touched my cheek to hers. I felt my arms wrapping about her, as if by doing so I could somehow encircle the pain and blot it away. I held her as close as I could. She willingly returned my embrace, her body relaxing, her arms reaching around me. Her face was hot from the drugs, from the cancer, from the fever. I pressed my cheek even more firmly into hers, moist with perspiration.

For that instant, I could share her pain, her worry, the fever that would not easily subside, her blood counts too weak to fight its onslaught. I could share her rage, her peace, her many rosaries, the days when air flowed gently through a full head of hair, the mornings she awoke to a tear-drenched pillow, covered with that same hair, now in clumps, lifeless, useless.

We released each other. I stood there, saying nothing, just looking down at her. "Please come back," she said. "Come again. Anytime." Her face was radiant, her eyes alive. She waved a goodbye.

Just down the hall, as I entered Room 802, a nurse was going through the medications the patient was taking. "Coumadin, Librium, Xanax, OxyContin." The list eventually reached eighteen. Curtis nodded at each medication. Lilly lay quietly in the bed, in a fetal position, her breathing hollow, eyes closed. He knew them all well; he had tended his wife lovingly.

"I'm going to die today." The words were barely audible. Curtis nodded again. Yes, she said it earlier that day and now again. This was the day she would die.

I prayed with them, broke off a small piece of the host, and placed it in the tiny space between her teeth and tongue. I gently touched her cheek and brushed her matted hair back on her temple. I gave the remainder of the host to Curtis. I stood quietly. Lilly's hand was resting on her hip. It was a beautiful hand, anyone could see that, even though the knuckles were swollen with arthritis, the fingers slanted at a ten-degree angle, the veins pronounced.

I placed my hand over hers and held it tightly.

Through those veins, I felt the pulsing of fifty-five years of marriage to this man at her bedside, three children, nine grandchildren, a life in upstate New York, laughter, tears, worry, faith, doubting, belief, anguish, happiness. I didn't know if her good heart would beat beyond this day, but for now I could feel it, strong and sure. And I could sense another heartbeat besides Lilly's and my own. It was her Savior and Friend, now within her, his own Sacred Heart beating with ours, all joined so we might sustain each other. Lilly, about to be united forever with her God, who had come to her in this most intimate of ways, giving Jesus' body for the sake of her body.

Early on I realized that everyone does not want to be or need to be embraced by a stranger. I knew to be careful of both touching a part of a patient's body that had just been operated upon and of the tubes and monitors that should not be disturbed. Then there were those who gave off definite signals that they did not want to be touched. I respected that. But I accidentally found a simple way that I might unobtrusively make physical contact with every patient.

At first I did it without thinking. As I was going around the bed of an elderly woman who had given me an extremely bad time, I didn't want the visit to end on a sour note. Her abdominal cancer was causing excruciating pain, her difficulties with a marriage gone bad, and a Church she felt had not helped her through either the illness or the divorce had inspired a tirade. I had said nothing in response but simply listened. She took the Eucharist, virtually snatching it out of my hand.

I don't know what prompted this, but I reached down and touched her foot, giving it a gentle pat as I passed by. That light touch, all I could offer and all that she might allow, was its own communion, a momentary entrée into her life.

And so this became part of my visits. Sometimes I squeezed or wiggled a big toe or patted the top of a foot. Sometimes I hesitated, my hand resting on the foot, saying something I hoped would help or silently offering a look of encouragement. At times, there was only one foot beneath the sheets. Gangrene caused by poor circulation and diabetes was the usual reason for the amputation.

Where had those feet—or the foot—trod? Of course I knew little of their lives. But if it were the welder who worked on the Verrazano-Narrows Bridge, those feet intrepidly navigated narrow beams of steel. One foot was propped on the foot rail of dockside bars, telling tales of wind and danger and red-hot rivets, of union meetings and old girlfriends and his time in the army during World War II. Those feet stood before the coffin of a wife who died much too young.

The foot of the songwriter whose lungs were clogged by years of smoking once tapped to the beat in a recording studio, a maze of cables and cords beneath him, joining guitars and drums, a slide guitar, amplifiers. Yes, those feet danced at the bar in Nashville they all went to when the last song was just right. Those feet, walking to the mailbox to find the album, his name in bold letters in the liner notes.

The farm wife whose feet I patted one morning, then only one foot two years later, then a few years after that two stubs, the diabetes relentlessly assaulting her body. Those feet walked the rows between cabbage and pepper plants as she hoed the weeds. Then she walked alongside Mexican laborers in the fields to fill cartons that would be shipped to supermarkets so many others could partake of the nature's bounty she and her sons had so carefully nurtured. Yes, and slogging through those same rows in high boots, to see the plants lank and brown, the beginnings of a bean or squash buried in mud. The crackle of frost-crusted leaves beneath those feet. A young girl, barefoot in soft spring grass in a sun-dappled pasture, ready for gazing, opening the gate to the eager cattle.

How honored I was to hear their stories during my short visits, with none of the incidentals of how much money they had made or titles they earned, but of the important moments and people in their lives. How God had touched them. How God seemed so far away at times. The miracles of love and friendship, the satisfaction of honest work, the heartbreaks. The distant sounding for whom the bell had tolled when they found they were not invincible after all, and a multisyllabic diagnosis would number their days.

In India, it is a sign of reverence to bow low, even drop to one's knees and touch the feet of a maharaja or spiritual master, to acknowledge one better, higher, more evolved than you and your station in life. And so I touched the feet of those who taught me, by words or merely a look, what life is and is not about.

How honored I was to touch the feet of these saints and martyrs who otherwise go unnoticed by us, but not by God.

First and Other Communions

Although I am about serious business—bringing God in the holy Eucharist to the sick and dying in a hospital—it does not mean that strange, humorous, and entirely unpredictable things do not happen.

I have given holy Eucharist to scores of people as they sat on a potty seat. I have caught them in the middle of brushing their teeth. I have lifted oxygen masks to place a host on an outstretched tongue between gasps for air. I have used liquids to help patients wash down the host, a few of which I believe contained a dose of Jack Daniels.

And, unwittingly, I have given first Communion to at least one patient—and certainly a second Communion to many others. The patient in Room 832 stands out in my memory. I shall never, ever forget Mrs. Gold.

She was a tidy package of ninety-odd years, a well-wrinkled face framed by stunningly well-shaded and coiffed blonde hair. Mrs.

Gold greeted me with a warm smile, obviously happy I had come and apparently well-aware of the purpose of my visit.

We chatted for a few minutes about happenings in our city, the muggy summer weather, a testy race then underway for one of our state's U.S. senate seats. She pointed to various parts of her body where either present or past operations, illnesses, infections, bursitis, arthritis, or aneurysm had held sway. While she was perfectly willing to talk, I hadn't found any personal points to connect with and go deeper into her life. This happens often enough. I reached into my little pouch.

"Mrs. Gold, I have Communion for you this morning."

"Oh, good," she replied, sitting up in bed, folding her hands in front of her.

"Lord, be with this good woman today, and as for those aches and pains—touch her with your gentle touch so that she will know you are here in the Eucharist, that you will be caring so lovingly for her all the day through. This is the Lamb of God…" I could see her eyes focused intently on the host I held before her.

"But only say the word and my soul shall be healed. The Body of Christ, Mrs. Gold." I placed the host on her outstretched palm. Then she did something very strange. She took a small bite, as if it were a cracker. She chewed, savoring the flavor, then took another small bite.

Flashing lights were going off in my brain: *Not a Catholic! Not a Catholic!*

She finally finished, and I tentatively asked, "Mrs. Gold, you are Catholic, aren't you?"

"Goodness no," she grinned, "I'm Jewish. But I believe in it all. I watch the evangelists on television, I go to synagogue when I can get out. It's all the same, don't you think? You know—God?"

Wars have been fought, millions slaughtered in the name of The One True Faith (fill in your personal preference), and here was Mrs. Gold leveling the playing field so God could range far and wide. *No, they are not all the same, Mrs. Gold,* I mentally stammered, *but yes, Mrs. Gold, there is only one God.* My head was spinning.

"Well, Mrs. Gold, I want you to know you've just received your first holy Communion."

"Thank you very much; that was wonderful." And with a radiant, beatific look rivaling anything that Thérèse of Lisieux or Hildegard of Bingen might have evinced, she pulled the sheets over her bony shoulders and reverently closed her eyes.

I hesitated in the hallway outside her door for a moment of reflection. What had just happened? Had I done something horribly wrong? I had just given holy Communion to a non-Christian, a person who not only did not know what the Eucharist was, but didn't even believe in the divinity of Jesus Christ. He was an honored son, but a misguided messiah, to Mrs. Gold. The hallway was unusually quiet, affording the blank screen I needed just then.

God is the God of us all. (Thank you for your at once astute and elementary theology lesson, Mrs. Gold.) I would have to leave the further complexities to God. I had no good answer. Except to think of it in terms of love—a spousal love that Christ demonstrated and promised. A love that unites, yet allows differences, allows each person it touches to remain intact, yet forever changed. And Mrs. Gold was now tucked beneath her sheets and her finely done hairdo with the comfort of a God both of us knew and were united with—only in slightly different ways. I had walked with her on her path to God for just a few steps, opening my little gunnysack and sharing the food I needed for my life's journey, food she eagerly accepted.

I knew I must be more careful. But I was not about to become the Grand Inquisitor, demanding baptismal certificate and concrete evidence that each patient was in the state of grace and therefore worthy to receive. Training for eucharistic ministry varies from diocese to diocese, sometimes even from parish to parish. My instructions had touched on certain criteria—regular church attendance, reception of the sacrament of reconciliation at least yearly, parish membership. But there had to be other ways to determine if I were talking to a "practicing" Catholic. Or not.

When I entered the room of an O'Malley or Dougherty and heard a Boston "faaathah" or the "ya know" of a New Jersey accent, I was reassured. With a southern accent, I was a little more cautious. Native-born Catholics in my part of the South were a rarity.

"Got you down as a Catholic; any truth to that rumor?" was my slightly askew, offhanded way of asking those whose accent gave away their birthright. But even this proved to be another gateway swung open. With just a little encouragement, I would hear of their early days in a Catholic parish or school, the Ku Klux Klan member who had no room for this brand of Christianity—certainly not followers of the same Lord and Savior as they—of their playmates who made fun of the Saint Francis statue on their front lawn. And then we could pray together, the transplanted Yankee Catholic and these, the native sons and daughters from below the Mason-Dixon Line.

Then there were those I visited who were of an era doubly—and truly—marginalized: Catholic and black. Still other gateways would be flung open.

Joseph's eyes were rheumy with age, his body rail-thin, his hands large, bent, and calloused. He had picked his share of cotton, followed a mule through miles upon miles of furrows, raised a dozen children, and lived to see dozens and dozens of grandchildren, great-grandchildren, and now a sprinkling of great-great-grandchildren. Today was shrouded in mist, but his tenant-farmer days were so clear: the dignity of hard work, the pleasure of a long row of okra and collards before him, choir practice in a tiny country parish where the roof always leaked no matter how many times it was repaired. The slights, the indignities this noble man had suffered, were far offstage as the final curtain neared.

"Dear Sweet Jesus, our beautiful Savior, you have been such a fine companion to this good man for so many, many years," I found myself praying, a different tone and cadence to my voice. "You hold him in your heart, you shelter him under your mighty wings."

"Yes, Jesus, yes." I barely heard his whispered voice, husky with throat cancer, yet so velvety soft.

"Let him feel you right here, Lord, right in this room today, his Savior come to his comfort once again."

"Yes, my Jesus, I'm awaitin' you. Jesus, Jesus, yes. ..."

For almost all of my patients, I offer an *a capella* prayer, but with black patients like Joseph it is call and response: the backwoods, evangelical duet of two supplicants before the altar of the living God, lifting up, encouraging, underscoring. I found I could pray longer, stronger, and deeper with black Catholic patients, for these are the crucified ones. They know the sacrifice of the cross. Each has been hung there, and many are still.

I looked at the host at the tips of my fingers, then at Joseph. Who could identify more with Jesus, be closer to him, than this man? Out of his pain—perhaps not spoken or even remembered now, but so etched on his soul—comes the truest prayer, purified and tempered in life's fires. These communions are written indelibly in my mind, these powerful moments with those who knew Christ of the cross and tomb so well, yet who knew his vindication and rising even better.

And then there was the first-Communion dilemma of Mr. Murphy in Room 724. He was as Irish as they come, with a shock of white hair and eyes all the bluer set within bleached, parchment-like skin. He looked at me quizzically as I asked him how he was doing, where he was from—the usual set of questions. He said nothing as I prattled on, so I knew enough to stop. I took out a host and said the prayers.

"I've never received before," he suddenly blurted out as I was about to place the host on his tongue.

I looked into those blue eyes. Just that he had used the word "received" was enough sign to me that Sister Mary Whatever Her Name Was had instructed him well many years before when, dressed in a fine wool suit and white boutonniere, he approached the altar rail for the first time. The dementia had taken away so many memories—including those of his first Communion— but Mr. Murphy held fast to at least a part of what he'd been taught.

"God will understand, Mr. Murphy," I said softly. "He wants to be with you today, so let's just let him have his way."

Signs and Wonders

While I am a firm believer in the Divine Presence among us, I do not see ours as an overstated, obvious God. Loving, yes. Overzealous and pushy, no. In other words, I don't believe God is constantly impatiently nudging us, sending signals that demand our decoding. As we muddle through life looking for evidence of God's presence, we might eagerly ascribe great significance to the strange way a leaf happened to fall on the hood of a car, the shape of a cloud, the discovery of a dollar bill in an unlikely place—the reading-the-tea-leaves school of revelation. We are little different from the apostles during Christ's time on earth; we of such puny faith are constantly looking for solid proof of God's existence and power just to make sure we are not trusting in vain.

But now let me quickly contradict myself: I see amazing and miraculous signs of God's presence all the time during my hospital rounds. I may be reading too much into what I have experienced.

However, there have been too many of these signs and wonders to be denied. Real. Powerful. Undeniable. Quiet. Subtle.

These signs and wonders make perfect sense, after all. Would not our God—without being overstated, obvious, or overzealous—want, in continuing yet understated ways, to communicate his presence to us—especially when we are most in need? I believe in a mysterious God who also makes sense, hardly a profound theological category. If God is indeed a heavenly Father and a phone call or e-mail message might not be his way, will God not find other ways to let us know God is with us?

As children, our simple and trusting faith reaches out unabashedly to God, tapping the deepest yearning that we have to be one with our Creator. We want to be understood, sheltered, guided, loved by that awesome power so much greater than we can hope to possess. Growing older, supposedly wiser and more discerning, our communication with God too often mutates from honest exchanges to convoluted negotiations. From God's side, I feel, it doesn't change. Uncomplicated, direct, searing messages wing their way in our direction. We look the other way. We deflect. We post rationality at the entrance to our souls.

Time in a hospital bed turns back the clock to our youthful innocence and hunger for God. We are once again open; there is no place for pretense. The wall is down, the gate thrown open. God is allowed in. Allowed into our lives in ways that continue to astound me, as I found out that morning in November.

The cardiac intensive care unit was unusually busy when I called from the red phone outside, asking permission to see the patient in Bed 3. Two cubicles were jammed with doctors and nurses, shoulder to shoulder, tending patients who had taken a turn for the worse. Cubicle 3 had no one but Elliot and a legion of electronic monitors keeping a running account of his every respiration, heartbeat, fluctuation in temperature, and a myriad of other bodily functions. He was heavily sedated, his glassy eyes partially open. I approached the bed.

I held the host in the air over him and said a prayer in a soft voice so as not to disturb him. It was not a long prayer, no more than a minute, if that. "O God, hold this, your son, in your tender embrace. For you are our Father in heaven, and you always seek our healing. Let him somehow know you are with him and will never leave this beside. Let this be a good and restful day for Elliot. ..."

As I prayed, his eyes held their sleepy stare, never moving, then closed slowly. As if a tranquilizer had taken effect. I thought no more about that visit until the next week when Elliot had been moved to Room 740. His hospital gown was low on his chest, and I could see the beginning of a long row of clamps and the incision, with a red tinge along its swollen boundary.

When I asked how he was doing, he was eager to tell me.

"You're from the Church, so you'll understand," he confided. "It was a terrible week after the surgery. I was in terrific pain, in and out of consciousness. They tell me they didn't know if I was going to make it. But then it happened." He looked about the room, to make sure we were alone.

"I was visited by this angel," he continued, "an angel of mercy. I don't even know why I call it that. The angel kissed my forehead. It rubbed my feet. I don't know how to explain it, but I knew I was going to make it through. It was the most profound religious experience of my life. I'm a little leery telling people, they'll think I was just delusional." He paused, looking at me to see if I believed him. Assured, he continued. "But it was real, so real."

No, I am not the angel of mercy, and I would not claim any credit for Elliot's experience. Other extraordinary ministers of holy Communion from my parish visited Elliot during those days. What did they pray? Did they hold the host over him? Kiss his forehead? I don't know. However, something happened to Elliot, of that I'm sure. God did come to him in the guise of an angel of mercy, bringing him comfort and the confidence that he was going to pass through this valley of darkness and into the light.

When I am alert and focused as I hold the host before sleeping patients and those about to receive, I can understand completely what Thomas Merton wrote about his profound experience at the ancient statues of the Buddha at Polonnaruwa, in Sri Lanka:

> I was suddenly, almost forcibly, jerked clean out of the habitual, half-tied vision of things, and an inner clearness, clarity, as if exploding from the rocks themselves, became evident and obvious...I don't know when in my life I have ever had such a sense of beauty and spiritual validity running together in one aesthetic illumination...I mean, I know and have seen what I was obscurely looking for.

So it is when God comes to us. The complicated is deciphered. What we have sought—without knowing, articulating, or understanding—is there before us, the answer to our unspoken plea in exactly the right form, with an action appropriate to the need.

On another morning, I was met at the door to Room 833 by a

gurney bearing the still form of Mrs. Sawicki. She could not have weighed eighty pounds. She must have been in her nineties, with lines etched deep into her forehead and cheeks, sunken now without her dentures. She was being taken for a test or procedure, and she looked close to death—her skin dry as parchment, a sickly grayish color. The attendant knew me and paused.

I prayed that God would guide the hands of the doctors and technicians and that Mrs. Sawicki could rest assured that God was with her at every moment. It was a short prayer; I try not to get in the way of hospital work and workers: "In the name of the Father and the Son." Her bony hand moved slowly beneath the sheet. It was obvious she was trying to reach up to her forehead and bless herself. "In the name of the Father," I began again, and the hand slowly made its way upward. I continued, as slowly as I could, "And of the Son, and of the Holy Spirit, Amen." Her eyes remained closed.

The gurney was moving down the hall. Instinctively, as I often do when I leave a room after praying with a patient and giving them the Eucharist, I gave her a thumbs-up. She was about to be wheeled into the elevator. The last thing I saw was that her hand had finally made it out of the sheets—and she was returning my thumbs-up. Ninety-odd-years old, eyes closed, and giving me a thumbs-up.

A sign of God's presence? Absolutely.

I have gotten to know many people who work at the hospital, one of them a heart-monitor technician who works for many of the cardiologists in our city. His job is to precisely set the rate of pacemakers, and he is legendarily very good at it. A cheery guy in his late thirties, he was leaving a room just as I was entering one morning. There was something he needed to complete his work on the patient in Bed 2 and sure, I could give her Communion, he said. He'd be back in a few minutes.

I spent those few minutes in the room with Ronnie, who must have been a tempestuous young woman, because now in her seventies, with flaming red hair, she still was a *femme fatale*. She had just had the pacemaker implanted and would be going home the next day. She confided how worried she was that it would work correctly. That was my prayer: That the pacemaker would hold the right beat for her good heart, because it was obvious that was exactly what she had.

The patient in the next room took quite some time, and as I was leaving, my technician friend was wheeling his portable EKG out of Ronnie's room, work complete. He stopped me.

"I—I don't know how to say this or explain it," he began. "Something was different when I came back."

At first I was worried. Had I disturbed Ronnie, mistakenly unplugged one of the leads he had carefully placed to get his EKG reading? He was a man with a perennial smile. The smile was gone. He was very serious.

"I felt the presence of God in there," he said. "She wasn't the same person after she received Communion. I mean, the heart monitor readings didn't change—it wasn't anything like that. But she was different. Calmer? Yes, I guess she was calmer; everybody's worried if these things really work. How do you figure things like this? I couldn't really explain it, and if I had to put it my notes I wouldn't know what to say." Then his smile returned.

We both knew there was nothing more to say. We looked at each other for a moment. Then he turned and went his way, and I went mine.

The pacemaker. The peacemaker. That tiny piece of bread that is Christ, ever so subtly, ever so lovingly, holding back the thin veil that separates us from God so that Ronnie might know God is there.

Praying the Psalms

On more than a few Thursday mornings, when I arrive at the hospital I feel a bit like the young boy who came up to Jesus, opened his little pouch, and produced five small barley loaves and two dried fish. It was his pitifully small offering in answer to a huge problem. Five thousand men—the addition of women and children probably quadrupled that number—were sitting on the hillside. They had traveled great distances to see Jesus and to hear him speak; now they were hungry. What could be done with this meager amount of food? His apostles scoffed. How could they meet the overwhelming need facing them?

I look at the long list of people I am to see on those days, some fifteen or twenty, occasionally even more. They too are waiting on the hillside to be fed, for each one will have a hunger. Some will be very sick. Some will not be able to say what it is that keeps them from God—from being fed with holy food, the Bread of Life—on this day. I may walk into a room and be told to leave immediately, that I am not welcome. I never know.

Jesus raised his eyes to heaven and prayed over the loaves and fishes that somehow there would be enough to satisfy the multitudes. I step into the small, windowless hospital chapel off the hallway just before the elevators, list in hand, and pause. I sit for a minute or two, focusing on what I am about to do. Then I go to the open Bible on a table beneath the stained-glass window on the front wall, dimly backlit by low-wattage bulbs. Usually the Bible is open to the psalms; it is obvious others have sought solace from these terse words. Wherever my eyes fall, I read a verse or two. On one particular day, the Bible was opened to Psalm 34.

As I reflect on the role of the psalms in the lives of so many people, across the religious traditions, I'm reminded of a conversation I had with Rabbi Jay Rosenbaum. I followed him for a year and wrote a book about that experience, *And They Shall Be My People: An American Rabbi and His Congregation* (Grove Press, 2000). Rabbi Rosenbaum told me that for Jews, reciting the psalms in formal prayer was only part of the psalms' power. The idea was to have the psalms floating through a person's mind, instructing, guiding, and tempering that person as she or he went through the day. That day, it was Psalm 34 that would be with me in the eighteen hospital rooms I visited—and strike with resounding resonance in four of them.

I will bless the LORD at all times;
    praise shall be always in my mouth.
My soul will glory in the LORD
    that the poor may hear and be glad.

Who are more humble than the sick? And who more than they want to hear good words and be glad? Such was not to be the case in Room 819.

His wife was standing next to him, outlined against the cold morning light. He sat on the bed, slumped over. He was wearing a pair of good cotton pajamas, not the usual hospital gown. They were both suntanned in the middle of winter. His wife's fashionable sweater set, a single strand of pearls, and huge diamond ring further confirmed their secure rung on the economic ladder. They were people who had everything. But all that changed minutes before I came into the room.

I was preceded by their oncologist. The CT scan showed spots on the patient's liver and pancreas. Although Byron had had no symptoms, the cancer had been spreading through these two vital organs for months. It would not be useful to operate; the doctor told Byron the cancer was too advanced. Chemotherapy would temporarily shrink, but not eradicate, the offending cells. The doctor didn't have to say more. Byron had just been given a death sentence.

Regardless of our accomplishments or our wealth, we are all humble in a hospital. Our bank account and hospital plan may buy us better treatment and single rooms like Byron's, but mutating cells or crumbling bones or a malfunctioning gall bladder are undiscriminating equalizers. Our mortal bodies march to a beat beyond our bidding.

After sitting for a while on the edge of the bed, my hand on Byron's shoulder, I took a host from the pyx and held it up to the ochre light. I looked at it and asked God to guide my words. "Byron," I began, "we can't explain how this happens, but he is going to be with you in the days ahead in ways you never could imagine. I've seen it over and over again. This is your friend, a friend you've called on before, I know you have." He shrugged his shoulders in tentative agreement. "He is going to open doors and paths. He is going to shatter all the false impressions you have of a distant God. He is going to come into your life so clearly and simply it will amaze you, overwhelm you at times. What happened this morning is terrible, let's not soft-peddle that. What is about to happen is a miracle."

I felt his hand moving along the smooth sheets. He covered my hand with his own. And he squeezed tightly.

The psalms are mysteriously relevant rays of light that seem to pierce the fog of our lives just when we need their insights. Psalm 34 itself is a prayer—a cry, really, even a wail—of thanksgiving, each line beginning with a successive letter of the Hebrew alphabet. It begs for rescue and protection, all the while proclaiming a deep trust in God.

Magnify the LORD with me; let us exalt his name together.
I sought the LORD, who answered me,
delivered me from all my fears.

What a bold thought, to deliver me "from all my fears" especially there in the hospital. And who would know more about fear than Randy in Room 734? Randy had been a volunteer at the hospital for many years, his flinty Marine Corps exterior poorly masking the compassionate man within. He had been trained as a SEAL, a band of the toughest warriors of them all on sea or land or in the air—or any combination called for. He had fought in Vietnam and been decorated for valor many times over his long military career, but there he was, burning up with a staph infection after surgery, his eyes darting back and forth, seeking relief from his agony. He knew if the infection was not controlled, it could end his life.

I held the host in the palm of my hand as I stood beside his bed. I paused and prayed. "Randy," I began, "you weren't a good Marine; you were a great Marine. But were you scared when you jumped out that airplane door, slogged through those rice paddies at night? You bet you were. But you were a pro. You delivered. You did what needed to get done.

"Turn that around now," I continued. "This God, this God who's been in your pocket all these years, who got you through everything, well, this is his time to come through for you. He's not letting you go through this alone. He's right there, your wingman. Quiet, sure. And he's saying right now, Randy, 'Let me carry some of the load. I can do it. I want to do it, because I love you, Randy. I love you, and you just aren't going to have to shoulder this one alone. Whatever it is, I can take it.' Hand it over, Randy."

Randy stared at me and said nothing.

"What kind of God do you think he is? We all wonder. What's he really like? Is he really in it for me? Just me? Now? Here? Let's think about that. When the going gets tough, when you're in a bad spot, what would a Marine—what would *you* do for a buddy, Randy? You'd give even more. That's him. That's the way he is. He's here for you, Randy. 'Whatever you can't carry, I can,' he's saying. 'And we're in this together. One step at a time. I'm here right now, and I'm not leaving you for even a second.' That's the kind of friend he is, Randy. We both know that, don't we?"

I placed the host on his tongue and straightened the neck of his perspiration-stained hospital gown. Randy closed his eyes. His breathing grew more regular. I stayed there for a few moments, but he didn't move. He was asleep when I left the room.

Look to God that you may be radiant with joy
and your faces may not blush for shame.
In my misfortune I called,
the Lord heard and saved me from all distress.

Cynthia. I had seen her far too many times on my rounds. She was a wife and mother, not yet forty years old, with three children in grade school, a Brownie-troop leader, and a diabetic. Unfortunately, her disease was not easily controlled by the regular injections of insulin that provide a normal life for millions. No, her diabetes was an unpredictable ocean, calm and placid one day, raging the next. She could be on a scouting trip in the morning, in intensive care in the afternoon.

Her face was flushed as I approached the bed. I could smell that characteristic sweet, alcohol-like odor on her breath. She slowly opened her eyes.

"Cynthia, we've got to stop meeting like this." I offered my somewhat shopworn but customary greeting. She smiled weakly. "Oh, Paul," was all she could manage. I had long before gone through the Litany of Unfairness, the Litany of Unfortunate Circumstances, the Litany of Errant Body Chemistry, the Litany of Regular and Irregular Diabetes. There was not much to say about her illness. All I could do was—and I use this term advisedly—behold the woman with a look that I hoped in some small way told her how much I cared for and admired her. For in that pain-racked face was a brave, uncomplaining woman who certainly did not court, understand, or deserve what life had dealt her but had somehow embraced it.

Finally it was time. I couldn't just recite the prescribed prayer; I knew that. "Cynthia, this is the Lamb of God," I began and found words I had never used before, "offered on an altar not of his choosing, to be sure. But offered, nonetheless, for each of us." At that she smiled; her eyes flickered open, then closed slowly. "Happy are those of us who are called to this, his eternal banquet. And what a rich and full banquet it is, Cynthia. He is here, with food that sustains us, food that lets us know that whatever goes on with our bodies, he refreshes our souls, revives our spirits, reaches us in ways we can't really understand, but we just know are exactly what we need. The God of the Ages, Cynthia, the Jesus who ate with his apostles, here in this room. For you.

"Lord I am not worthy," I began, then stopped. Even though this was the proper prayer, how could I go on? "Lord, this is Cynthia. You know her so well. But please say that word," I then continued with the proper prayer, "but only say the word and I will be healed. This is the Body of Christ." Cynthia didn't open her eyes, but her mouth opened a crack to receive the host.

How could I describe the look on her face then?

It was as if Cynthia knew, beyond the boundaries of rational understanding, beyond the reach of medical science, beyond anything of this world that, at that very moment, she was healed. There was no doubt in that lovely calm face, none whatsoever. I had come to bring sustenance to her. But it was she who brought it to me.

The angel of the Lord, who encamps with them,
delivers all who fear God.
Learn to savor how good the Lord is;
happy are those who take refuge in him.

Bill was my last stop in the medical intensive care unit. A likeable Irishman from Staten Island, New York, he had been away from the Church for decades, decades that had seen him earn a good living as an ironworker on bridges, raise a family, and eventually lose his beloved wife of almost fifty years. He had been through tough times before, close calls scrambling over the narrow girders, a tour in the icy wasteland of Korea's demilitarized zone, and most recently a depression that had stalked him since his wife's death. He was friendly enough, believed in God, but no, he didn't need religion; he would tough this one out too. Been through it before.

Might I say a prayer? I asked. Sure, he allowed. I took a host from the pyx and held it before him.

"Lord, here is Bill. He talks to you all the time, doesn't he? Maybe not in Church, but that's not what counts. You know him. He knows you. That's not hard to see, just by the kind of guy he is. But this is a little different now. He's hurting. His body, yes, that's hurting. But it's more than that. You know better than I do. He's not a guy to ask for pity or special treatment. So let *me* put in the request. Just let him feel you are here, Lord. That you are with him in a special way. Right now. Whatever way that is, we'll leave that up to you, Lord. And Bill will know, as sure as anything. He'll know that you are reaching out to him, like an old friend, saying 'Come on, Bill, come back to Me. I've been waiting. When *you're* ready, Bill, I'm ready.'"

A buzzer on one of the monitors went off in the next cubicle, its insistent, staccato bleeps demanding immediate attention. Bill stared at the host. Then at me. Then back at the host. "I'll take that," he said, a man, who once he made up his mind, never hesitated to act.

My rounds were over for this Thursday. I turned into the first-floor corridor and walked slowly toward the main entrance. Visitors were coming in the opposite direction, flowers, bags of donuts, or a favorite fast food in their hands, loving intentions to meet the needs—spoken or not—of their loved ones. As I walked past the chapel, I paused for a moment outside the doors. Psalm 34, read two hours before, had traveled with me, to come alive on the floors above.

My Choir of Saints

A few blocks from the hospital is a new, small building with twelve rooms clustered around a courtyard where tropical plants flourish and goldfish swim in two lovely little ponds. Each room looks out onto its own private terrace—a perfect setting, most who visit here will say. But for those in the twelve rooms, while it may be an idyllic setting, it also marks their final appearance on the stage of life. This is the hospice unit.

Some weeks I have no patients in hospice, other weeks two or three, and as I make my way from room to room I am struck by both the brightness of the place and the grave condition of its residents. When I first visited over a decade ago, I found myself walking slower, speaking lower, almost afraid to smile or offer a remark—hopefully on target and, if intended to be, mildly humorous.

But the dying educated me to stop this faux-sympathetic posturing. Some patients I visit may be in pain that medications cannot entirely control and some are angry about their illness or their life; but more and more I began to see that these were but stages on the way to a threshold most achieve before they pass on.

When I enter a room, the patient is often lying quietly. Often there are pictures of loved ones around. There might be colorful notes from grandchildren or great grandchildren displaying the optimism of the very young, wanting Grandpa or Great-Grandma to get better. There might be a wedding picture. They look so young, so hopeful. He with his proper suit and slicked-back hair, and she almost lost in the cloud of crinolines, her rosebud lips crinkled in a smile. The soldier with the bride he is about to leave to fight on a beach in the South Pacific or the French coast at Normandy. Her modest wedding dress and tiara that might still be in a trunk somewhere. Faded pictures but clear memories, memories of what once was.

Now as they look to the future, there is no promise of getting better. No more bargaining. No next, more powerful medicine. No miraculous, cutting-edge procedure. Earthly promises and hopes fade.

As I received my education at these hundreds upon hundreds of bedsides, I learned that most of them come to realize this is but a passing moment, that an even greater future awaits them. It is called eternity.

I enter these rooms to usually find the patients still on their beds. I look first to the face, then to the sheets or blanket. There is no dramatic movement, so I wait and watch. Yes, an almost imperceptible movement. Up…a hesitation…down. The shallow breath of the dying, the limited oxygen taken in by a body whose organs, diseased or simply worn out by age, have lost their synchronicity, the rhythm of life that mysteriously and unobtrusively sustains us. We know it has been there all along only when it starts to falter.

While the body starts to fail, the soul opens up to God clearly and magnificently. I compare it to a rain falling on the hard soil of our indifference and lack of faith, a rain that runs off when we are healthy and consider ourselves hardly in need of God's presence. Little is taken in—the rain evaporates before it can do any good.

Broken soil, on the other hand, hungrily drinks in every drop of a rainfall, and so do broken, sick, dying bodies. God is able to refresh us with love and graces simply because we are defenseless to stop God.

I talk to the patients who are awake, not with platitudes about the healing power of the Eucharist, for in these cases it will not, cannot—actually *should* not—heal a body that has run its course and wants to return home. No, I use words in prayer something like this, either to the patient, or to family members who might be there:

"Dear God, you are holding your beloved one so close to you right now. And you are speaking to her in words that we don't hear, but she hears so clearly. She hears your voice, so warm, so reassuring, so welcoming. And she is speaking to you as well. No, we don't hear that either. But *you* do, every word. She knows you. You know her better than any of us in this room, and you know the beauty of her soul, the richness of her life, the sacrifices she made for others, the love she has for you. Let this be a peaceful and pain-free day for her as we hold her just as tenderly as you have held her all her life and will forevermore. We are so fortunate to be with her now and with you, present in the Eucharist. Thank you for all you have meant in her life and ours. Amen."

I have spoken with enough hospice patients to know that God

does speak to them as they lay dying, and they speak to God. The threshold they are upon is not marked by a discreet line between life and death, but a floating zone of consciousness and unconsciousness, of being here on the earth, there in heaven. For dying itself is not only a biological moment, a heart stopping its beating, brain waves flat. It is a marvelous, grace-filled process where God gently orients the dying to their real life, introducing godliness and eternity with such appeal that departing this world becomes entirely natural. "It was a pleasant enough sojourn, but home I must go." How many stories we have all heard of the reluctance of those who "died" and were brought back to life? The sweetness of what is to be beckons.

On a few occasions, I have been especially blessed to walk into a hospice room, and after waiting for the rise and fall of the sheets or blanket, find there is none. They have crossed over the threshold. I am the first person to know the patient has died.

So it was one morning with Philip, a distinguished former Fortune 500 corporate executive I had visited a few times.

I stood at the foot of the bed before Philip's still body. There he lay, hair perfectly combed, his thin hands folded on his chest, as if he were taking a nap. The sheets were perfect—not a crease, just as this fastidious man would have them be.

Philip, I thought, *You are seeing what we all yearn for—the face of God. You are there with him. Philip, please intercede for those of us still on earth thrashing around. We are trying to sort out our lives, and we are so venal, so human, so frail, so magnificently stupid at times. But now you see all that, see in a way we can only imagine. It all makes sense now. After all, he did keep his promise to prepare a place for you.*

Philip, I know I can always call on you, that you are with God and you will always hear me. But right now, before so many others know you are gone, please help this one human being live in way that is pleasing to God. Help me not to give in to my impatience, my rash judgments, my sense of entitlement and superiority, which I try to mask with false humility. Help me be worthy to carry him in the Eucharist to patients here and at the hospital, that he will pierce the doubt we all have with the brilliant light of his presence. Thank you, Philip.

Looking back, I see a choir of saints throughout these years at the hospital and hospice. What a rich and varied lot they are, with little earthly similarities, yet everything important in common with one another.

The Vietnam veteran I visited so many times in the hospital and then stood before him at home, sitting there in his recliner as if he were about to talk to me. His wife called that Saturday morning, and I came right over. What a privilege to be there with a man who had fought in a war and then fought drugs so bravely and then came back to the Church and the Eucharist to die in peace in God's loving care.

And Elizabeth, whose husband asked me to deliver the homily at her funeral. I knew her so well, this elegant lady who died with such dignity, her makeup perfectly applied. An excellent mother and wife, she never asked for pity, but always inquired how everyone in the room was doing, what was in the news. Even as she grew sicker and sicker, it was hard to believe such an indomitable spirit would not go on forever.

Some of the precious babies I saw are teenagers now. A few never left the hospital alive—what heartache for their parents. But there they are, with the God who would hold them so carefully and well.

They didn't have to live decades to be brought home. God took them in his due season, not ours.

I treasure this choir of saints I have come to know in a place where death seems to prevail. I carry them with me and know that whatever the need or the circumstances of my own life, someone will understand. I never leave the hospice unit morose or sad. It would be a disservice to those within.

Finally, It Is About God

As I look back over the record of my weekly visits to the hospital, I find little notes to myself in the margins of the lists of room numbers and names. These notes are about God—the power of God a patient felt, the peace of God another experienced, the trust still another knew that was not misplaced.

There one such scribble in the margin of my morning notes on a dry, breezy July day, a welcome respite from the heavy midsummer weather we experience in my part of the country.

When I entered his room, I was taken aback by the clump of blood-soaked bandages at his right ear—pooled, caked blood in every crevice. George's face told another story. He was clear-eyed, with that small smile of the recently anesthetized, waking up in pain but relieved the operation was over. His face was gaunt, but the fine wave of hair—a very 1940s style he had never altered—rose up from his forehead, freshly combed. If lipstick and mascara are signs that women have the will to get better, a combed head of hair serves a man's statement of intent.

We chatted a bit about his name, Polish sounding with a -*ski* ending, and we traded some anecdotes about the ethnic parishes we had each been part of. He was Lithuanian, but when his parents arrived at Ellis Island the quota for immigrants from Lithuania had been filled. Poland's quota had not, so they were quickly recast and respelled.

I took a host from the pyx and began, "In the name of the Father and of the Son and of the Holy Spirit, Amen. Lord Jesus Christ, great healer that you are, place your hand upon George that this surgery will heal quickly and well." I realized George was speaking too, softly and barely audibly. Oftentimes, people will follow my prayer, repeating even these spontaneous prayers, word for word, time delayed, a wonderful echo, rendered twice to God.

"Thank you, God."

He said it several times, and it was his tone I remember so clearly. It was not the prayer of the ardent, repeated like a mindless mantra, again and again, or of the supplicant, seemingly thanking but really asking. It was the prayer of someone who knew the presence of God in his life for over seventy years, felt that closeness still again, and didn't want the moment to pass without acknowledging it. *Thank you, God.* Unadorned. Straightforward. Direct. George was a man who knew God as a friend.

"This is the Lamb of God, who takes away the sins of the world. Happy are those who are called to his supper."

"That is so beautiful," he said at the end of the prayer, of these words repeated over and over every day across the globe.

I smiled at him. What could I say? I have said that prayer many times, sometimes with feeling and sometimes so routinely I am ashamed.

"We'd be lost without him," George said, after he swallowed the host and took a sip of water to ease his Savior through a dry mouth.

Yes, George, we would be lost without God. This mysterious God of the ages here again this July morning, for you, George. Present here as this wafer of bread. Standing at your bedside, his hand in yours. We of the Catholic Christian tradition, George, for whom the Eucharist is central to our bodily and spiritual lives, are humbled by the greatness of this gift. Has God not always been there, George, with both of us, when we welcomed God and when we turned our backs? Yes, George, so lost.

I couldn't speak those words. They would have come out all wrong. Too sincere. Too moist. Too pietistic. As I touched George's foot and left the room, our nod to one another was enough. He knew that I knew exactly what he was talking about.

I knocked on the door of Room 630 to find a woman standing there. Her husband was taking a shower. I told her I would come back and asked if she was Catholic. She was Baptist. "Same God, last time I looked," I offered my standard reply. She smiled. "Sure is."

When I returned, Norberto was in the bed, his wife seated next to him. He was lying flat, the sign of some orthopedic procedure. He grimaced as he repositioned himself and said, "God is so good to us."

In my prayer, I prayed if not his exact words, his sentiment: "God is so good to us."

It's strange. I rarely use those kinds of words when talking to Catholics, but with a Baptist in the room I felt more at ease. And Norberto surprised me: "When you accept him as your Savior."

These words, of course, are stock in trade of the evangelical churches and not of my own. They tell of a personal encounter with the risen Lord and turning one's life over to God. Those words are not in our Catholic lexicon. We're a bit more reserved. We do not talk about being "saved," but rather about adhering to our Church doctrines and practices and, hopefully, turning to God each day with the intent to live a better life, closer to God's Way. Norberto, raised Catholic and who reverently received the Eucharist, had obviously been influenced by the faith of his wife.

And so I am once again humbled—and educated about the power of God. Norberto's faith was so strong, so sure. When we are bodily healthy, we of the Catholic tradition—who have the living Christ daily available to us in the Eucharist—might take God into our bodies, but often we haven't taken God into our hearts.

Not in the hospital. For here, the well-fortified beachhead of our intellect and rationality is useless against the onslaught of pain, worry, desolation. And here God comes to us so sweetly, so openly. Just to see a bandaged or palsied hand trembling as it reaches up to the forehead to begin the Sign of the Cross, is to see a perfect act of faith, a perfect acknowledgement of our relationship as daughter or son to the heavenly Father.

Denise, who I visited in Room 817, was an emaciated woman with darkened bruises covering her body but wearing such a radiant look on her face I found I almost had to turn away from its brilliance. She did not readily volunteer her medical history, but as we talked it was slowly revealed in horrifying detail. Failed kidneys, a pancreas transplant, both prednisone-weakened hips broken in a fall, Coumadin turning her skin a palate of sickening colors.

"God...God," she began. "He has been so close to me through all this. How can I say that I'm lucky all this happened so I could see that?" She laughed at the thought, motioning to the two metal intravenous trees bearing bag after bag of the medications that would keep her alive another day. "Would I rather be healthy? Of course. I didn't ask for all this, and he didn't do it to me. But what a friend he's been. What a wonderful friend I never knew before."

Are there such people with this outlook who are nonbelievers? Yes, I have found a few who endure their suffering well, consigning it to the fickleness of our bodily mortality without a trace of outward religious belief. God surely embraces believer and nonbeliever alike—how else could it be?—and I can know only what I see or hear in the short time I am with my patients. I wish all nonbelievers would allow God into their lives because God could do so much for and with them. I want them to know they are part of the Body of Christ regardless of their doubts, skepticism, or sheer lack of interest.

The awareness started so slowly, but over the years, going from room to room, bringing God in the Eucharist to these thousands of patients, I began to understand that oft-stated religious phrase that had always been so many words to me.

The Body of Christ.

In theology, depending on varying interpretations, this concept embraces all Catholics, all Christians, all the world. I subscribe to the third choice. And the Eucharist is the most intimate manifestation—at least in the tradition I know best—breaking through boundaries of time and mystery, the God of the Ages, the Christ of two thousand years ago soaring across the centuries to be present in the circumstances of an individual's life.

Week after week as I would place that tiny consecrated host in an outstretched palm or on a tongue, I began to sense this was not an isolated act known only to God, this person, and me. It was a ripple that would be felt in every corner of the world, God's wonderful presence experienced here yet radiated throughout humanity, a tiny drop of grace added to the magnificent, ever-replenishing ocean of love. All those other members of the Body of Christ—old, young, of all cultures and countries, all within the divine embrace—were made all the more capable to live their lives, to bear their burdens, to pass along their blessings because of what was happening in Room 924 or 513, in the intensive care unit or hospice.

Four thousand personal visits from God and Christ and the Holy Spirit among us. Four thousand souls nourished. Four thousand hearts assured of God's unwavering care and concern. Week after week I was among those slow-witted and confused apostles who encountered Christ on the road to Emmaus, recognizing him only in the breaking of the bread.

And now, this journey among the sick of soul and body, those dying, those who already passed on, ends with grace—Grace, actually.

She stood at the entrance to the cubicle, the patient within barely visible beneath the tubes and lines that both kept him alive and monitored just how well modern medicine was performing. "It's not the patients that wear you down," Grace, my intensive-care angel said, leaning against the wall. "It's this place." It is a common enough complaint with hospital workers that "they," the administration, just doesn't understand. Their efficiencies and mandates often seem to stand in the way of good patient care. "I need it today," she continued, putting her hand on my arm.

The *it* was the Eucharist I carried in that now-worn black pouch at my waist, and I offer the Eucharist to hospital staff like Grace, a veteran intensive-care nurse. Fresh-faced nursing students, physicians, staff—over the years we have come to know each other, and these hallways serve as our parish church on Thursday mornings. But Grace would be the first to agree that it is not only this place but everywhere we need the *it*—the presence of God in our lives, the knowledge that God hears our cries, that God comforts and encourages and invigorates us to lead the lives we know we are meant to live.

I stood with Grace and began to pray. "Lord, Jesus Christ, we live in an imperfect world. Sometimes it is so hard to just do what is right, what is needed. We pray too for the administrators of this hospital; sometimes we don't realize they are doing their best, although," I squeezed Grace's hand, "it just doesn't look that way. We put ourselves, all of us, in your hands at this moment, in this day. For you are the way-maker, you will show us how to live in your image, to make this world a better place because we have been here. Now be with this good—no, this excellent—woman Grace, and let her feel you right at her side and that you will be there all through this shift and her life. Make the way, Lord. We know you can and will. Amen."

I placed the host on her tongue.

Grace took a deep breath, held it, and exhaled so that I could hear the soft whoosh of breath. She bowed her head, then looked up at me. A smile crept over her face, like ink saturating a blotter—or better put, grace saturating a soul.